Country Ways

A Country Year in Hampshire, Dorset & Wiltshire

Also available:

Country Ways
A Country Year in Kent & Sussex

Country Ways

A Country Year
in Hampshire, Dorset & Wiltshire

ANTHONY HOWARD

Countryside Books/TVS

Country Ways
is produced for TVS by
COUNTRYWIDE FILMS LTD.

First Published 1991
© Text Anthony Howard 1991

COUNTRYSIDE BOOKS
3 Catherine Road
Newbury, Berkshire

ISBN 1 85306 150 6

Front Cover Photograph by Neil McIntyre (Swift Picture Library Ltd.)
Back Cover Photograph by Martin King (Swift Picture Library Ltd.)

Black and White Photographs by Tom Howard
with additional photography by Derek Budd (pp 6, 9, 13)

Line drawing by Pip Challenger

Colour Photographs:
Dennis Bright (Swift Picture Library Ltd.) p54
T.D. Codlin (Swift Picture Library Ltd.) p36
Rod Cooke (Cameraways Ltd.) p71
Mike Read (Swift Picture Library Ltd.) pp17, 72
Andy Williams pp18, 53
A.J. Wren (Swift Picture Library Ltd.) p35

Produced through MRM Associates Ltd., Reading
Typeset by Acorn Bookwork, Salisbury
Printed in England by Borcombe Printers, Romsey

CONTENTS

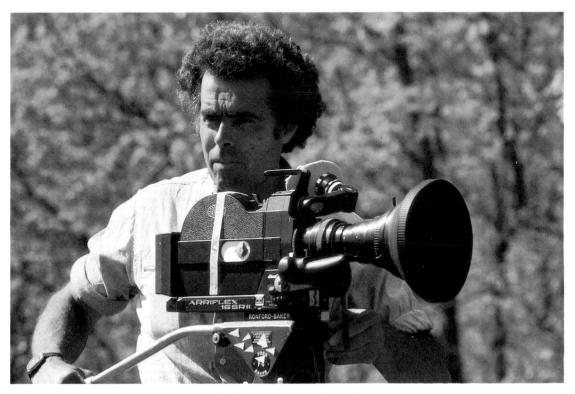

Anthony Howard, the Executive Producer of *Country Ways*.

'There are afternoons when the rooks waver and caw over their beechen town and pigeons coo content; dawns when the white mist is packed like snow over the vale and the high woods take the level beams and a hundred globes of dew glitter on every thread of the spiders' hammocks among the thorns. And through the mist rings the anvil a mile away with a music as merry as that of the jackdaws that soar and dive between the beeches and the spun white cloud ... The end should come in heavy and lasting rain ... And then, after many days, the rain ceases at midnight with the wind and, in the silence of dawn and frost, the last rose of the world is dropping her petals down to the glistering whiteness and there they rest blood-red on the Winter's desolate coast'.

EDWARD THOMAS 1879–1917

INTRODUCTION

NOWADAYS, it is hard to remember when people started to be concerned about the countryside and the effect upon it of human behaviour. The word 'green' has been hijacked and has lost its honest meaning in the bitter political arguments which rage about the natural history, the wildlife and the fields, rivers, woods, hedges, skies and coastline of Britain. Everyone today claims to be a conservationist – even those who for years have been dumping poison in the rivers, wrecked cars in the woods, tin cans in the village streets and cigarette packets on the roads. But there is as much hypocrisy spoken on this subject as there is about wage rises and inflation by the leaders of industry. Old habits die hard and the pot has been calling the kettle black for a long time now. There is no limit to man's ability for self-delusion.

My impression is that most people started caring about the countryside during the 1970s. What is curious is that the concern often seems to have turned into the sort of ignorant aggression that usually does more harm than good. The green land of England is torn by rows and riven by arguments while the people who, over the centuries, have cared for and cultivated the country have stood back bewildered and confused while the chattering classes have usurped their role and stolen their clothes. Men and women with their roots deep in the British soil and whose ancestors had, in their millions, and through many generations, helped create the landscape which we know and which so many of us love, were suddenly ignored, treated with contempt and told by people who considered themselves to be their betters that they knew nothing and were destroying the places they most cared for. Quiet and considerate as they so often are, they backed off quietly and watched the newcomers with a mixture of amusement and disdain.

WITHOUT wishing to boast about my prophetic powers, the first time I worked on a film on this subject was back in 1965. In those days people still walked rather than rambled and the earth's friends were everywhere. Rural England was largely untroubled by flower power and the exotic creatures of the decade. Only the odd pop concert disturbed the tranquillity. The film was called 'The Persecuted Forest' and told the story of Hampshire's New Forest and the invaders from the cities, who were beginning to threaten its peace and trample its lawns and woodland. It was before the days of lager louts and loads-a-money, but some gentle citizens from the towns were already beginning to use New Forest ponies as moving dart-boards and to ride their heavy-tyred bikes over the fragile surface of the ancient hunting grounds. It was time to try to support the local people against the savages. The star of the film, after the deer and the foxes, the badgers and the barn owls, was undoubtedly veteran forester, Fred Winter from Fritham. Red-haired and hard-eyed, firm-lipped and full of fun, his is one of the best known faces in the area. He was showing us one of his precious cows, which had been hit by one of the careless or couldn't-care-less motorists, who throng the narrow lanes where the animals roam free. Fred was standing by the stall while his wife was inside trying to manoeuvre the animal so that its rear end and the wound could be seen by the film unit. 'Get its arse round towards the camera', bellowed Fred in his strong, Hampshire voice. Ever obedient and thinking he was speaking to her, Mrs Winter slowly turned her back towards the lens.

With his rough ways and often harsh words Fred, and his ancestors before him, have done more for the New Forest than all the committees and interfering outsiders pooled together. It is in his interest to keep the place alive and unspoilt: 'I was born in this village and I come from commoner stock. My father turned out animals on the Forest before I did. And so did his brothers. And my grandfather, he turned out stuff all his life. I remember in this small village when there were nine or ten people producing milk and the lorry would come around and collect it. There isn't one left now. They bring it into Fritham today from outside, which is sad, I think. It robs the place of its personality. Anyway, everything changes I suppose – usually for the worse. But us old commoners, we stay much the same. We carry on making use of our rights on the Forest. You've either got to own some rights or rent some rights before you can turn your cattle out. And you have to pay up each year to do it, whether it's ponies or cows. The old agister, who keeps an eye on the commoners' animals, he comes round every year and collects the money for the animals and ear-marks them. He counts the ponies you've got and, whatever number it is, you pay for them. And that's how it's been going on for hundreds of years, and not changed much either. I'm fairly typical of the way small farmers have been here since way back. I couldn't live without the Forest. I've not got enough land. I've got five acres of my own and I rent thirty or forty acres, which is not enough to make me a farmer. Just sort of peasant size really. But I simply class myself as a Forest Commoner and I rely on the Forest to get my bit of bread and cheese. We don't make no money out of it. It just about pays its way and keeps ticking over. That's all it is. We only earns enough to pay the bills and keep going, and then perhaps you've got some over for Saturday night for a couple of pints when you takes the old woman out. If there ain't nothing in the kitty, then you've got a night in. That's our commoners' troubles.'

One of the virtues which has disappeared from our civilized world is the comradeship which binds communities together. It still exists in poorer countries where village life depends upon it and where the grandmother is still a more important member of the family than the new-born baby. People help their neighbours even if it is only because they may need help themselves one day. Some traces of this ancient goodness still survive in Fred Winter's community: 'During the summer months, when the animals stays out on the Forest all the time, we only goes out to look 'em over once or twice a week – maybe more if you're feeling like some company from them. But you see the system works because every night there'll be one commoner amongst us out on the prowl, because we'll all have our animals out. And, if I was going today looking over mine and I saw one of my neighbour's beasts sick or hurt, I'd do something about it. If I know he's away at work I should bring it in for him. If I knew he was at home I should come back and say to him, 'Look, you've got an old cow up there sick.' Then we goes up there together and gets 'un in. You helps one another, which is a great old custom I think and it's still going on today, which is as it should be. It's something you wouldn't find in many other parts of the country I doubt. Like yesterday, I was just going to have my dinner when one of the other old commoners rung up and said. 'A mare of yours is on the Green. She's had a foal, but it's not long to live. So we went up to have a look and found it. But it had already died. A nice chestnut filly it was. Couldn't be thirty-five or forty pounds. Could have saved its life him coming to tell me. Another time it may. But there it is — just one of the things we have to put up with. We've had the mother for four years. Then the foal dies. Being a young mare she probably won't have another one this year. So one way and another we'll have to keep her and feed her for six, maybe

Derek Budd, *Country Ways* camerman on location.

seven years before we get anything back from her. That's four we've lost this year now. But it's just one of those things I suppose.'

FILMING and talking to men like Fred Winter is of more value to me than listening to any number of lectures from academics or speeches from politicians. Here, if you are lucky, you come close to the reality which has made the world work and survive since man came down from the trees. The wisdom of such people is not from their heads but from the experience which has been handed down to them from their forefathers. Often they are unconscious of it. But, in the way they read the wind and the weather and in the instinctive lessons they learn from the behaviour of animals and birds, anybody spending time with them is aware of it straight away.

THE great county of Dorset is a film-maker's paradise. It breathes antiquity and its hidden corners are still exactly as Thomas Hardy found them over a century ago. Probably they are the same as they have been for many hundred of years. As with Fred Winter in the New Forest, there are men and women here whose lives reflect the land they live in. Charlie Pitcher is one of them. He is an old farm worker from the village of Long Bredy in the Valley of the Bride, which stretches in green glory behind the great bank of pebbles called the Chesil Beach. In all his long years Charlie has never strayed more than a few miles from his house. He has had a hard-working life and his face and hands show the signs of it. But his eye is undimmed and his spirit is unquenchable. Out ferreting in the winter mist with his grandson you can still see the boy he was early in the century as he flattens himself to the ground listening for the sounds of the rabbits below or when he springs across the burrow-filled bank to retrieve a ferret which has poked its nose out of one of the holes. Charlie believes that there is nothing special about himself or about his way of life. But that is where he is, for once, wrong: 'It's all changed a bit now – not always for the best. Tractors for horses is one of the main things. Then there were seven or eight of us working on the farm – and now there's only three. In spite of that, we used to keep thirty or forty cows them times. But now I should think we've gor a hundred and twenty on the same ground. Scenery's not altered much though. Nor for a while before my time I should guess. It's good steep hills and green banks, which give the horses some tidy exercise when the hunt's out. And I don't suppose that side of it has changed too much for a lot longer than I've been alive. I've lived in the Bride Valley all me life. I was born down the bottom of this village and I've lived here ever since. Worked on the farm all me life – same farm and same boss. I've been a good worker, I like to think. I've worked hard and I think that's about the main thing. Always been happy enough. Never been late for work in me life. Because I like to be early in the morning and early at night. I don't like to be hanging about. I always like to be on time. And I never worry about anything. Whatever happens, I don't worry about it at all. Don't do any good fretting, do it? The house I'm in, my Dad bought it about seventy-five years ago. I must have been two or three years old at the time. He gave £150 for it and he could have had the one next door as well for £100. The farmer he worked for would have lent him the extra money, but he wouldn't borrow it. He said he would never be in debt to anybody. Otherwise he could have had the two houses for £250 – and that would have been worth some money now, wouldn't it? This is a good village because it's hardly grown at all in my time. I think where village life has been spoilt, it's been because they've built scores of new houses and swamped the places with newcomers. I hope this one will be all right for my granchildren. They and all the other children in the village call me 'Gramp'. It's like that because it's small. We're ever so close as a family and as a community. I got three boys and we all live here together and mix in together all the time. My grandchildren and the village children, they're all my friends. Wouldn't be the same if it were bigger. There's two little girls – no relation at all – live up the street. It's always 'Gramp' every time I see them. I like kids and I've always had 'em round me. What will spoil it all will be if they put in the new sewer. At the moment, they aren't allowed to build any more houses. But if they put a new sewer in, I suppose they'll build right down into the village and beyond. Then they'll ruin it for sure. We get these people coming round that want to buy these houses. They don't mix in with the village people. We've got one or two of 'em now. They're higher up than what we are, I suppose. But you can't allow it to worry you – just so long as they don't spoil the place. So many villages now people don't feel safe in any more. Here I never lock the door when I go to bed or anything. Door's never bolted and people can come in and out as they please. When I go to work, I leave the door open and, if anyone wants to get in, they can. Rosemary always comes down and gets the fire lighted for me when I come home at night. I sets it in the morning and she comes in and puts a match to it. That's how village and family life should be.'

The streets of Long Bredy are grey and glistening on a damp winter's morning as Charlie trudges up the hill to work in the farmyard, which is only two minutes walk from his home. The Bride river – little more than a stream here – runs swiftly beside the road. The grey-stone cottages stand back, private and silent, behind fair-sized gardens. Rooks call and a cow bellows from the steep bank behind the farm. In the yard the farm cat, large and self-important after a busy night searching for mice, comes forward to be picked up and petted. Soon Charlie's boss, Robert Foot, who inherited Manor Farm from his father, arrives to sort out the day's work. He is a young man, quiet and shy, with none of the brash self-confidence which has become so much a part of modern agriculture: 'About 1913 grandfather bought the place. And we've been farming it ever since. First my father and now me. Charlie's been here nearly fifty years I should think and he's part of the furniture of the farm really. I can't think of a time when he hasn't been around. I've always known him, all my life and he's one of the good ones, the sort that's probably been working this valley ever since it was first cultivated. He's loyal and he's conscientious about his work and, from what I hear, that's rare nowadays. You don't have to tell him to go and do something if there's a slack hour or two. He'll always go off and do something or he'll come up and suggest what might want attending to. I might tell him to go and roll a field or to fix a hedge that's broken down and off he'll go. Doesn't matter what it may be. He does a complete job too, rather than coming back every five minutes to ask questions. Then he sometimes sees something wrong or which needs replacing or renewing. And he'll go off and get it done. The next day, before he goes off in the morning, he'll tell me there's some new barbed wire he's put up in the fence or that there's a wet patch in one of the fields which needs draining out to sea. He's always drawing my attention to these sort of things. He walks the farm more than I do and so he keeps me informed. He's as much a part of the place as the hills and the river. Times are changing now, of course. But he's always there and as solid as a rock. He's a good friend and I've learnt lots from him. Like how to get on with a job good and steady and not to rush around at it. Charlie keeps going at an even, steady pace and he seems to get the job done as fast as someone going in top gear and getting puffed out five minutes later. I suppose I've been watching him at work ever since I was a boy and that's how I've learnt so much from him. Those days, when I was four or five years old I suppose, a favourite trick Charlie used to play on me involved the exhaust pipe on the old tractor. It stuck out of the top like a chimney and the shed we used to keep it in was a bit low. So they used to lift the pipe off to drive the tractor under cover. And Charlie used to see me coming down from the house and they'd wait for me to come in and then start the engine with a bit of throttle. It sounded like a lion it made such a noise with no exhaust on it, and it used to frighten the devil out of me. So I used to run back home to mother, and I could hear them all laughing behind me as I ran. But I soon came back down again.'

ONE of the great pleasures of making films is having the chance to visit and see places like the valley of the Bride and to meet men like Charlie Pitcher and Robert Foot. It takes great wordsmiths like Thomas Hardy adequately to describe such countryside and such people. Here is Eden Philpotts in 'The Spinners' on this special part of Dorset: 'Bride river winds in the midst of the valley and her bright waters bring life to the cottage gardens and turn more wheels than one. Then westward she flows through the water meadows, and so slips uneventfully away to the sea, where the cliffs break and there stretches a little strand. To the last she is crowned with flowers and the meadow sweets and violets that decked her cradle give place to sea poppies, sea hollies and stones encrusted with lichens of red gold, where Bride flows to one great pool, sinks into the sand and glides unseen to her lover.'

Charlie might not recognise his beloved countryside in that rather exotic description, but his feelings for it – its past and its present – are no less intense. As always though he is rather more down-to-earth: 'You need to see it all the year round to get a real feel for it. Not just in the spring and the summer. You have to see it like the sheep or the cattle do – or us farm workers. In the bad weather it's rough and hard here. But that lets you appreciate the good times even more. You need to see it all hours too like we used to when we was milking cows in the old days. We always used to milk in the stalls them times, and they was all tied up at the back in pairs. We weren't milking more than forty, but it seemed a lot I can tell you when you were doing the job by hand. That's how it was when I first started and before we had the milking machines put in. All round the yard was rough those days. Just the bare ground and stones – no concrete or anything like that. I had to clean out the whole cowshed with just a wheel-barrow – push all the muck out by hand. Right in the middle of the yard was a great heap and we used to heave it up onto that and then, every now and again, we'd have the horses in and cart it all away onto the fields. Always had plenty of good working horses those days. I think I preferred it then. Life was quieter and surer, even if the work was slower. You seemed to have plenty of time to do everything. Now it seems to be a rush all the time. Of course, there was less than half the cows to milk that we have now. We used to just rear enough calves

Farmer Ernie Tee and his family with the film crew at their home at Denmead in the Forest of Bere.

to carry on the next generation. But we bring them all on now, a lot for beef and the rest to replace the diary herd. Before, we only used to keep the good ones. My very best memories of the old days though are when I was a boy. Long before I started work, when my Dad used to work in the woods making hurdles and fence posts and things like that, I used to go up there with him and try and help him out. He had an old donkey and he used to load the cart up with his wood and I used to look after the pea and bean sticks and haul them round for him. He used to make his hurdles up in the woods. I started doing it too for a while. But I found the work too hard, too rough on me hands. His hands were so tough that they were all cracked open, like bark on a tree. I've seen him put shoe-maker's wax in the big cracks and sew 'em up with a needle and thread, where they'd split open. He cut his arm one day and the nurse couldn't sew it up with her needle. She broke it while she was trying to. He was just like leather because he was always out in the woods, you see. Then in the summer he used to thatch the corn ricks and the hay ricks to keep the weather off of them. I did a little bit of thatching with him too. I've done quite a few ricks myself. But I never really took to it. Preferred to keep my feet on the ground. We went thatching a barn one time. I was only a boy and I used to carry the reed up to my father on the ridge. It was so high that, when I got halfway up, I just dropped the bundle. I could go no further. I either had to drop it or fall off meself. No, the best jobs for me were ploughing or hedging. Then you could get away up the top of the hill on your own and think your own thoughts. Used to do it all by meself up the hill behind the farm years ago. Just you and the birds up there. I've always liked to work on me own.'

Back in the New Forest, the daily routine is equally hard for Fred Winter and the commoners. It has to go on no matter what surprises the weather may throw at them. Animals have to be fed and watered and, more important still, have an eye kept on them. There is no room here for fair weather farmers: 'We work until dark if we're busy and, if I want to take a day off, I do. That's the glory of the job. I just work one thing in with the other. I wouldn't be much good at having someone tell me what to do. I've got an old house cow. She keeps us going with milk. That's another form of freedom if you like. We has what we wants and then the calves have the rest. There's no point having the milkman call, is there, when you've got your own? That's the idea and the beauty of our job – to have all your own stuff, your own grub. Mind you, it wouldn't suit everyone, specially not the tourists who come here in the summmer. Nowadays they're herded up in the Forest like a bunch of Commanches when they get here – all car parks and camping sites and marked walks. I always remember one who came by when I was out there milking the old cow one Sunday morning. The bloke got out of his car and looked into the barn and said, "Farmer, can I have a drop of milk?" And I said, "Well, I can't sell you none. But I'll give you a drop." 'Cos you aren't allowed to sell it, you see. Well, I asked him if he'd got anything to put it in. And he went to the car and came back with a big plastic bag. I can see him now with his dickie bow-tie on. He had a trilby hat on his head – a real city slicker. He had enough powder and scent round his ears, I could have sprayed three cows with it. So he give me this old bag and I squirted some milk out of the cow into it and give it to him. And he said, "I don't want that, farmer. It's orf. It ain't no good. It's warm. I can feel it."

So I said, "I'm bloody sure it's fresh, 'cos it's just come out of the cow this minute. And, if you don't like it, you can bugger off somewhere else and stop wasting me time." And he dropped the bag on the ground and away he went without a word. That's why city people don't always have a good name in these parts.'

MEN like Fred Winter and Charlie Pitcher are the life-blood of 'Country Ways'. We have met and talked to hundreds of them over the years. By the high and the mighty they are considered to be small people and of no significance. But, without them, the English countryside would not stand a chance. I doubt that any such claims in any area of life can be made about the great and the good.

SOMERLEY

SOMERLEY, a couple of miles to the north of Ringwood in Hampshire, has been the ancestral house of the Earls of Normanton for six generations. It stands on the edge of the New Forest in 7,000 acres of beautiful farm and parkland overlooking the river Avon. This famous salmon water winds its leisurely way through the Estate adding charm and dignity to the distant views of the great house. In January 1958, Christopher Hussey visited Somerley for 'Country Life' and wrote: 'Perched on the high west bank overlooking the Avon's water meadows, Somerley is in the strip of Hampshire between the New Forest and the Dorset border. In the valley below lies Moyles Court, with Ellingham church at the river's edge; upstream, beyond Fordingbridge, Breamore; both more ancient houses with which the manor's early history is linked. . . . Summerley, "water-meadow": the charming name is matched by the idyllic setting, typical of Hampshire beauty. Upstream the long drive crosses the river and, before climbing the steep wooded bank, skirts walled kitchen gardens at its foot. There, on the site of the gardener's cottage, stood the old manor house of Somerley, until its remains were demolished in 1803–11. An 18th century engraving shows it then as having Flemish gables and a tall order of pilasters in the front: a building of the kind termed artisan classical and suggesting a date of about the middle of the 17th century'.

Surprisingly little has changed today. The terraces and gardens at the south front still command distant views of the New Forest and down towards the coast. The house itself, built between 1792 and 1795 from designs by Samuel Wyatt for Daniel Hobson, a Manchester industrialist remains intact within the additions made in 1850 by the 2nd Earl of Normanton and in 1870 by William Burn for the 3rd Earl. And the surrounding landscape is as grand and gracious and impressive as it must have been for a hundred years and more. Great trees shade the handsome meadows. Pheasants hurry across the grass, and coots, moorhens and even sometimes a kingfisher dash and scurry along the river, where great swans glide.

LIKE many stately homes, Somerley has had to come to terms with the realities of the late twentieth century, and today Lord and Lady Normanton run the house and its land as a business with the help and participation of their talented staff. The pheasant shooting is classy and syndicated. The salmon fishing is among the best in England and beats are hired for appropriate prices. Film and television companies can use the house and its grounds as exotic locations, and makers of commercials or magazine advertisers for selling their wares. Lord Normanton has few regrets about this non-stop activity, which is vital to the survival of his family home: 'Somerley has been in the Normanton family since the mid 1700s. I think when a house has been lived in for all those generations it's bound to be a special place to me and my wife and children. In addition there's the fact that a lot of people on the estate are tenant farmers. Some of them have been here since my grandparent's time. A lot of them started with my father. So we have the potential historically of forming a great, big happy team. I was born in the house and have lived here all my life, apart from six years when I was away in the army. So it truly is a family home to me – even if it might seem a bit imposing to somebody looking in from the outside. I was bred and brought up to live in it and to look after it. I suppose I see myself as something of a guardian of the place really. Hopefully, one day, I shall be able to hand it on to James my son. With that in mind in this modern day and age we have to be commercial in order to keep it going. It really is not cheap to run and to maintain a house this size nowadays. So I am prepared, within reason, to do anything that is feasible to let it continue, so as to be able to hand it on as intact as possible to the next generation'.

ONE of the longest serving of Lord Normanton's tenant farmers is Tommy Sampson. His great-grandfather came to Hartbridge Farm in 1882 and the family has been there ever since. The farm is hidden away down rough tracks at the back of the estate and makes few concessions to modern ways or methods. Amidst a tumble of battered barns and rusty machinery, and surrounded by muddy yards and a much-used duckpond Tommy keeps the old traditions alive by using magnificent heavy horses to do much of the farm work: 'We've always kept horses. We use tractors for the heavy jobs. But what horses can do best, that's what we use them for. I've worked with them all my life and I've always had a great affection for them. I learnt to shoe when I was a boy with our local blacksmith. We've always had to know the how of doing everything with them. And with all that experience behind us, it seemed a shame to let it all go. So we decided to hang on to the horses. They've always worked in very well with the mechanical side. We can tackle both. We bred one batch in the early 1950s and then again in the '70s. The ones reared in the '50s lasted into the '70s. Then we took a stallion and that resulted in the present team of horses we've got today. People sometimes say that it must be awful hard work doing all these jobs with horses. Well, to be honest, I wouldn't know. We've always done as we've always done, so I can't tell the difference. But I'll tell you one thing, I don't have to take sleeping pills when I go to bed. I always sleep because I get tired. But I don't think it's any more exhausting than other farm work. I have no idea how far I've walked behind them. I've never counted the miles – but quite a few hundred I suppose. Though we don't always walk. Some of the old implements have got seats on them, the hay-making ones especially. Sometimes we sit sideways on the horse's back. It's with the ground work that you have to walk behind. But there's a good thing about that because it's usually done at a time of year when it's not unpleasant to get some exercise. You don't feel the cold walking behind a team of horses, I promise you'.

Coltsfoot grows in hard, bare, sandy places and on shingle. Shakespeare's description in *The Tempest* could have applied equally to the beach or to the striking plants:

> 'Come unto these yellow sands,
> And then take hands:
> Curtsied when you have and kiss'd –
> The wild waves whist . . .'

Swan Green in Hampshire's New Forest sits snugly between Lyndhurst and Emery Down. It boasts a fine cricket pitch with a short boundary, so watch out for sixes if you are passing by.

It is dawn on a grey January morning. The frost is still on the grass and Tommy's cattle are waiting to be fed. One of the great, iron-grey horses is swiftly harnessed to a wooden cart. Straw bales are piled high and Tommy sets off precariously towards the meadow along rutted farm tracks. Ice cracks on the puddles and birds scatter in alarm. When he reaches the beef animals the horse makes its own way in a steady circle over the grass while Tommy stands on the load cutting the strings of the bales and throwing the barley straw to the hungry beasts. Soon there is a long contented row of breakfasting cows, which Tommy looks carefully over before heading back to the farm like an ancient charioteer: 'The breed of these horses is percheron. They're strong and they're fast and they originally came from the Perche region of Northern France. We had Shire horses up till 1948 I expect it was – or 1950. And we had to make our big decision then. Either we had to get out of horses and onto tractors. Or we had to try both. Well, I'd always had a fair-sized tractor, which would do the really heavy work. So we decided then to change the breed to percherons because, although they're big and strong, they're also very good at trotting. With a rubber-tyred cart we could keep up with whatever we wanted to do as fast as we could with a tractor. That especially goes for things like feeding the animals in the mornings. Horses are just perfect for that. And the tractors get on with the heavier jobs. So we've found that the two things work well together. The horses are low cost too. Quite cheap fuel – a lot cheaper than diesel anyhow. And the harness lasts well if you look after it properly. What's more, you don't have that huge cost at the start, especially if you've bred them yourself. We're so pleased with the way it's going that we're training my son to work with them as well now'.

Out in the field behind the farm house three of the great, dappled horses are chained to a plough. It is a leaden winter afternoon. Rooks flap quietly overhead and settle in the leafless trees along the headland. Tommy commands his team to walk on, the muscled haunches take the strain and the plough bites into the soil. The pace is surprisingly brisk and Tommy's voice is constantly encouraging, cajoling, warning and scolding. The shares cut straight and true and gleam as the earth slides off them: 'We reckon to do what ploughing we can during the short days of December, January or February. We do all the animal feeding in the mornings, then take the horses in and get them ready. After, we plough through the afternoon and up until dark. Then in the spring when the ground is firmer we can do what's left with the tractor. But that's another plus for the horses because, on a lot of our ground here, we can't use the tractor during the winter time because of the softness of the fields. You only need one bad spot to get the tractor bogged down. Three parts of it may be dry. That's alright. But if the far end's wet, or the middle or anywhere else you just can't make any progress. You have to wait till it gets dry. With horses though you can get through practically anything without any fuss or trouble. But they're useful in all sorts of other ways too. This is a mixed farm – big dairy once but now arable and beef. We have calves, which we either

Lord and Lady Normanton run their house and estate as a thoroughly modern business, which will keep their land intact for future generations.

sell on or fatten and then there's about eighty to a hundred acres of corn each year, which we sell. So there's always something for the horses to be doing. And if ever we're at a loss we can use them for training. There's a project which we're part of to enable the lads that go on Youth Training Schemes to learn about horsemanship. It's useful because a lot of big towns and cities with parks are going back to horses for clearing up leaves and for gardening. They're more economical and a lot quieter than motor vehicles. But they're understandably having difficulty finding people who can work with horses. So this is something which the Shire Horse Society has started with the support of the British Horse Society. Between the lot of us we hope to be turning out the heavy horsemen of the future'.

It is the back end of the afternoon. The light is fading fast as the team comes back from the field. They tower above their master as they turn into the yard. The chains jingle and the great hooves strike sparks from the flints. Three massive heads bow in unison over the iron rain butt beside the stable and they drink long and deep. One at a time they finish and, like old men leaving the pub before closing time, they turn and snort and head for the warmth of the barn and the sweet smells of hay and oats: 'One funny thing I've noticed about ploughing with horses is that the gulls won't ever follow the horse-drawn plough nowadays. You can have a tractor working in the next door field and it will be surrounded by seagulls. But not one comes anywhere near us. Perhaps if it's a weekend and the machinery is not on the land, a few may come to us. But it's rare. It's almost as though they don't realise that what we're doing is exactly the same as the tractor with the same good results for them. It may be something to do with the man walking behind, though that didn't seem to bother them in the old days. It seems as though they've forgotten about horses and don't associate them with this kind of job any longer. Tractors plough and horses don't. One thing tractors certainly do is to get the job done more quickly unless they break down or get stuck. But another value of doing it with horses is that ploughing is a good job for training colts on. It's repetitious work and, after a young horse has been put with an experienced team day after day for two weeks or so, he becomes manageable and disciplined. Gradually then you can put them between the shafts or fit them to any other kind of job. As for us, we reckon by now that we can deal with most things that might go wrong whether it's harness breaking or a horse getting frightened and perhaps bolting. We've been at it long enough now to know how to tackle most things. With experience you can generally judge what might happen before it does. Mostly, if something goes wrong, it's a young horse. With our older fellows, they'll always obey. If we tell them to stop, they will stop. But with a young horse you have to take precautions – particularly if there's a chance of it getting scared'.

Night has fallen and a tawny owl calls from a tree behind the barn. Lights shine from the downstairs windows of the farmhouse, where Tommy is having his tea. The stables are dark but, from within, there is the comforting sound of the scraping of hooves as the weight shifts from one leg to the other.

BACK at Somerley a meeting is in progress. The room is warm and comfortable and decorated with dried flowers. A long table runs the length of the room with chairs ranged down either side. At the head sit Lord and Lady Normanton, their backs to a good warm stove. Flanking them are the chef, the butler, the secretary and two gardeners. There is an important shooting party arriving for the weekend. The guests are also staying overnight, so everything has to be carefully and meticulously planned and every detail of the work shared. The hope is that such groups will return to Somerley in the months and years ahead and that they will pass the word around and encourage friends and colleagues to follow in their footsteps. Lady Normanton is in charge of what goes on inside the big house: 'With everybody indoors and outdoors on the estate we have twenty-five people on our staff. That includes keepers and their boys. It's a lot of people to be responsible for and it's most important that everybody feels interested and involved in what's going on. Martin for instance is the chef and has been for the last six years. He came to us from a local hotel and he's wonderfully artistic and creative when he's producing his delicious meals. We've worked up a good relationship I think over the time he's been here. And I believe he enjoys it because he can express himself in his cooking. He can do anything from a grand dinner for a hundred to a supper party for four or six and right on to our own everyday food here or in the nursery. We work the menus out between us. If we have been out and have had something spectacular I come home and tell him about it and then he tries it out on us. Equally, if he comes across a new recipe which he likes the sound of, he has a go at it. The big challenge for us is that each year we try and have a whole new set of recipes because the same people come back again and again and we want to offer them something different each time. That means keeping records too of course. There was a time when I used to help with the cooking. But I don't enjoy it all that much to be honest and I think that, to be as good as we have to be and provide the quality we aim for, the job has to give you pleasure.'.

Upstairs the main dining-room, awash with silver and crystal, is being prepared for sixteen guests. Each place has a mat with an N in the centre and the crest of the Earls of Normanton. Crisp white napkins stand sentinel and beautiful, rough silver birds and beasts shelter the salt and pepper. A man in a black suit moves solemnly from chair to chair adjusting, straightening, polishing – making everything perfect. In a few hours the big cars will start drawing up on the gravel in front of the house: 'John looks after the house for us. He is the butler. He is Italian but he also speaks French, Italian, Spanish and German, as well as English of course. It's wonderfully useful because we have a lot of foreign guests who need help and advice. He's been with us for two years and is very hard working. Nothing's too much trouble for him and he cares for the house as if it was his own. You can't ask for more than that really. Then outside we have two gardeners. Rob runs the main garden and looks after the greenhouse and the flowers that come into the house. Brian does the herbaceous borders and also looks after the kitchen garden. He produces all the wonderful vegetables that we cook and the herbs which Martin uses in his dishes. The flowers for the house are terribly important. I love to have the rooms full of colour. My husband always says he needs a machete to get into the house. But to me they are terribly important. So, a bit like in the kitchen, we are constantly producing new plants and flowers that can be used indoors. In addition, the garden's open two or three times a year so we have to keep it in good order. I do all the flower arranging myself. It takes me quite a time but I very much enjoy it. Rob does all the plants inside. He and I choose the different bulbs and things at the beginning of the year. To me they bring a room alive. Without them it is quite dead. A bit like I feel about meals and fresh vegetables. I do insist upon them. I think it's valuable from the health point of view. It's important to me for the children to be brought up on vegetables out of the garden. They taste better and you also have more of a choice. We can grow things that you can't always buy, especially in the country. It's difficult to get unusual things from a local greengrocer. So all in all it's a busy life. But as long as your energy level is high, it's wonderful. Obviously you get tired. You're occupied all the time and that's stimulating. It helps enormously that I can share it with my husband. He does the estate side and I concentrate on the house and garden. But we're bouncing ideas off each other all the time. It wouldn't be such fun without having that two way communication and support. We get great pleasure from the fact that we are keeping something going that we both feel very strongly about and love'.

Lady Normanton is a classic English beauty – tall, blonde and elegant. The inside of Somerley matches her and reflects her taste. It is the kind of house where you find new and surprising excitements in every room. And the views through the big windows are a constant reward: 'I don't think when I first came here that I realised what a big undertaking it was going to be. Fortunately we were both young and had a lot of energy. And my goodness we needed it. So the business side of our lives has just grown and grown, almost without our realising it. Before we came, my mother-in-law lived here on her own and I think she found it quite a burden. There was nothing going on the commercial side and we just had to do something to keep the house in the family. So the shooting, the filming, the fishing, the seminars, the courses, the rally-driving – everything has grown from there. But the important thing is to keep one step ahead all the time. There are pluses and minuses about it for us personally, but I think the pluses win. We can improve the house, for instance. Each year we try to do up a bedroom or to achieve something with the furniture, to have some pictures cleaned or to add a bathroom. Then we have the benefit of having the staff in the house, which we certainly couldn't afford otherwise. I suppose the main difficulty is with the family and never being on your own – that's what I find hardest of all. But having said that, we do live a privileged life and we are very lucky in our team. We couldn't possibly manage without them. Each is as important as the other and it's vital for us to keep in constant touch with them all so that we can try to understand their side of any problems with our guests, clients and visitors. In the winter that means shooting parties coming from America, Austria or France. Then in the spring, summer and autumn we have fine art courses and garden courses. They stay in the house for a week. There's always the fishing too. And also people come and take the house for a day for business entertaining and that kind of thing. So I've always got to appear at the door to welcome them as if my days had not been at all hectic. And then the children rush around wondering where you are and what you are doing. That's the hardest thing of all, trying to share myself between the children and the business side. Obviously I'm lucky that the work is at home. But quite often when I feel they need me and that I should be with them I've got to say I'm sorry but I must go and look after the guests. That means that the children miss having a story read to them or game played with them, which is sad. But they gain as well I hope by meeting and talking to lots of different kinds of people and seeing things and hearing about countries which they never would otherwise'.

The lights come on in Somerley as darkness falls. The last jobs are done and the fine tuning is finished as the first members of the shooting party draw up outside. A busy weekend has begun for Lord and Lady Normanton and their staff.

JOHN Staley is Lord Normanton's head keeper. Originally from Gloucestershire, he is now in his fifteenth demanding season at Somerley, where he is in charge of everything which concerns the highly sophisticated and developed skill of rearing pheasants for the men who queue up and travel huge distances for a day's shooting on the estate: 'The one thing I can't do anything about is the weather. I often wish I could. Unfortunately this year it's not been too good at all. We've had very wet days and the poor old beaters have been wet and cold. I think they're quite pleased that we're coming to the end of the season. It's a long, arduous task for them and for the loaders, the dog men and for the keepers as well. We do something in the region of thirty days shooting each year – that's wild fowl days, the big commercial weekends with double guns, the smaller, syndicate days and on to the shoots for friends in January time. Overall we've not had a bad season at all and the birds have flown well despite the wet weather. You just have to make the best of the difficulties and to look ahead to the good weather which is bound to come along sooner or later. Somerley is excellent for shooting. I'm bound to say that, aren't I? But it's true nonetheless. I've been through a lot of estates in my time and there are some first-rate ones around. But here we can offer all aspects of shooting. The birds off the high banks, the woodland birds, wild fowling, deer stalking, spaniel and retriever trials, clay pigeons – everything. And then you've got the beautiful Hampshire Avon running through the centre of the estate and that, added to all the rest, must make it one of the most beautiful places in the country'.

The frost and mist are still on the watermeadows as John and his team get ready for the day's shoot. The keepers wear smart tweed uniforms and tweed caps. Their faces are trim, wise and weathered. They have keen eyes and are as alert as the dogs which bound about in their excitement. The beaters are a more motley crew but every bit as cheerful. They favour green or khaki and sport heavy rubber boots. They cast pessimistic looks upwards where the clouds are beginning to gather. The first Rolls Royce draws up in the yard outside John's handsome house as a flock of white doves settles on the roof: 'The guns that shoot here have mostly been coming for some years now. We know them as friends, which is as it should be. They all know what they're doing. Some are better shots than others of course. But they're all safe and we know we can trust them to do their job properly while we get on with ours. The beaters are a good crowd too. There are eighteen or twenty of them that come religiously every shoot day two or three times a week. Our oldest is 87 and he's a marvel and then there are some teenagers who come along as well. Lots are working men, but there's a surprising number of professional people too – from banking and commodities, solicitors, lawyers and so on. They all come along here and look forward to a day's beating in the country. Not for the money but for the friendship and the fun of the shoot. What we aim for at Somerley is the quality of the shooting rather than the quantity. The more difficult I can make it for the guns the more pleased I am. And they like it that way too. So the windier it is on the day the better it is because the birds fly that much faster and that much higher and thus present more challenging shots to the guns. At every shoot we have eight guns. Normally that means six standing in front of the drive and one walking either side. With them we have four to six pickers up. They're a good crowd. One of them was in the Indian Army and is over seventy but he comes loyally every time. Then there are the dogs as well – every breed but all well trained – labradors, spaniels, pointers, retrievers and so on. And we the keepers try to organise it so that it all runs smoothly and as calmly as possible. Once the shooting season is over of course our job changes. Then we have to catch up hens and some cocks to produce next season's birds. We have catching pens in various woods where we feed them. We bring them home and put them in laying-pens. We put a tape round their wing which prevents them flying away. Then they stay here until we have enough eggs for incubation and hatching. We are completely self-sufficient at Somerley and rear all our replacements ourselves. Afterwards we clip the tapes and let the birds go back into the wild. But they still come along for food and water in the woods. In return they give us plenty of eggs. Then the young birds grow through the summer and autumn and the whole cycle starts again at the start of the shooting season'.

The last drive of the day is over. Men and dogs are tired and muddy. A small spaniel struggles through the choppy waters of a lake with a big cock pheasant in its mouth. Weary legs take the strain up steep banks as they head for the vehicles which will take them home. John Staley blows a long blast on a short metal horn. The sound echoes through the woods. Above the moon is bright in the winter sky.

Alan Jones' smile testifies to his pleasure in his work as river keeper on the Somerley Estate.

THE Hampshire Avon is one of England's greatest salmon rivers. Alan Jones, the river keeper at Somerley, has been tempted South from Staffordshire to look after and run this magnificent sweep of water. He has fished all the famous rivers of Scotland and now he is in charge of the fishing and of everything else on this fine river for Lord Normanton: 'All estates have a feel about them and this one is no exception. You fit in with the sort of estate it is. We're lucky here to have a tidy set of rods to fish. The river is excellent too – perhaps not up to the best Scottish ones, but super spring salmon. The best one we had last year was 33 pounds. Quite a lot of very heavy 20s too. While we don't get hundreds of fish we still do well. And the rods that come here are really looking for that super specimen – the 30 pound plus salmon which everybody wants to get. If you can catch them in surroundings like this, what more can you ask? You can go to other waters perhaps with more fish. But there might be roads running alongside and traffic whizzing past. Most people would think that there's a little more to fishing than catching salmon. You have to combine first-rate surroundings with top fishing and that's what we've got here. It's a complete day out for any fisherman. I'm extremely lucky because Lord Normanton allows me a day's fishing every Wednesday. When I say every Wednesday, that's if circumstances allow. If work has to be done, then work has to be done. But I certainly try to get it done on other days so that I can fish on Wednesday'.

Alan is a bluff Northerner with a strong face and the sound of the high country in his voice. He is stalwart, heavy-booted and wears a tweed hat and plus-fours. He is a strong man with keen, experienced eyes which seem to be able to watch the river and to know what is going on beneath the surface: 'It's one of those rivers that runs through meadowland and so there are problems with soil erosion and with silting up. That means we have a permanent maintenance programme with bank rebuilding and structuring the river. The thing you must do is to keep it all as natural as possible, even if you're diverting water to prevent flooding and building up places to save meadowland. You're trying to make homing pools for salmon and at the same time keeping everything as good as it's always been. There's no end to the work. Each flood varies. It takes some banks out, leaves some behind and changes others completely. A pool can be altered out of recognition overnight, so you have to be on top of the job all the time if you're going to keep the fish coming up and the fishermen happy. In principle we have two types of salmon. There's the spring fish which are heavy when they're working their way upstream in the early part of the year. They like to be on smoother water. So we try to make the pools they have to work when moving up have heavy water followed by easy water. The easier it is, the smoother it runs. So the ultimate for us is to get heavy, turbulent water coming into a pool where there's then a smooth piece. That's where we hope the salmon will lie for the anglers. Then in the summer we get small fish – anything from six to nine pounds. They are the type of fish that like the faster water with more oxygen in it. So for them we want the pool structures into smooth water, fast water and turbulent water and hope out of each stretch of water to get the best of salmon fishing. And I hope we succeed. Coming down here from the North I've been pleasantly surprised, though I did have some fears initially. As I travelled down by car the the road got busier and busier and my anxieties greater and greater. But when I found Somerley estate and took a look at it, it was like an oasis in a desert. It's quiet. It's peaceful. It hasn't got the hurly-burly and I've found that I can be happy here. We haven't got the volume of people pressing in on us out here that most people have in the South. There's great pleasure too in working on a great river and knowing that your little contribution will benefit it now and in the future and that it will still be flowing down to the sea with your additions and improvements hundreds of years from now. Add that to the scenery and the surroundings and you've got a job in a thousand'.

THE great salmon lines flicker and flash as the long rods propel them across the shimmering surface of the water. A heron drifts clumsily overhead as it heads downstream towards Ringwood. Somerley stands proud and with dignity in the middle of its precious patch of England.

EMERY DOWN

THE small village of Emery Down sits close to the west of Lyndhurst, the 'capital' of Hampshire's New Forest. Few guide books mention this far-flung hamlet, concentrating as they do on the greater importance of nearby Minstead and of Lyndhurst itself. Yet places like Emery Down are typical of the Forest, which, in April, is slowly coming back to life after the dead winter months. Ponies are at last finding something to eat other than gorse and brambles. Rhododendrons and azaleas, which flourish on the poor heathland soil, will soon be starting to show. And the wide expanses of the thousand year old hunting-ground are beginning to lose the drab brown of their Winter coat and to assume the greens and greys and purples of their Spring splendour. Poor though the land is, this is countryside to be treasured and protected, standing as it does in its wildness less than two hours from London and closer by far to the thousands of people in Southampton, Portsmouth, Bournemouth and Basingstoke. It has often been described as a lung for the city-dwellers of the South-East. But, like any lung, it is delicate and can easily be clogged and destroyed. It was the last home to scores of Canadians, who camped in the woods above Emery Down before D-day and then died on the beaches of Normandy. Their families and friends remember them here still and have erected a simple, wooden cross in their memory.

JACK Newman from Acres Down Farm is a New Forest farmer and commoner, who keeps cattle, ponies and pigs out on the open forest as his ancestors have done through the centuries. He also keeps a mixed flock of sheep and their young lambs in muddy meadows close to the farm house. This is not good farming land and people have to scrimp and save to make a living. But the true old commoners who remain seem willing to put up with the hardship in order to enjoy the freedom which their chosen way of life offers them: 'I was born in the New Forest at Cadnam seventy-three years ago. When I was nine years old I went to Bramshaw farming with me father. Then, in 1945, I started out on me own at a farm down by Minstead Church. So I've not moved far – about five miles in all. This New Forest is important to me all right. It gives us farmers grazing rights and a lot of other ones as well. And I wouldn't want to see any of that change. Trouble is some things are changing too fast already. I'm slowing down though now I'm older. I walk round the Forest, take me time and appreciate it even more than I did when I was a young man. I notice a lot more things going on than what I used to. After all these years I think I know every tree round here. And every pond and patch of soft ground. It's not just walking either. It's going out to look over your ponies and other animals to be sure they're all right. It's not easy for us Commoners to make a living out here. There's a lot of hard work on poor land. You go up to Wiltshire – just a few miles away – and you'll find the ground is totally different to what it is round here. For us and our stock there won't be no food really until about June when the cattle starts to do all right. They're my main thing really – the beef animals. We've got about a hundred and fifty head of them. And, in the mornings, you can set your watch by the time they come in off the Forest. They're here regular at quarter past eight to go and have their food. I let them stay in until one or two o'clock in the afternoon. Then let them back out again. The next morning they're back again regular as clockwork. One thing you don't need to worry about 'em for is that they get plenty of exercise. Some of them go from here to Brockenhurst six or seven miles away. But usually, at night-time, they wander off about three or four miles. They've just got their natural run and they'll cover more or less the same circuit every time. Come May, of course, they run out permanently from then till October. They've got their own haunts and they'll stay around those areas all the time. It's never too difficult to find them even after several weeks. But they will stray six or seven miles from the farm, but always to the same sort of places. That can be a worry for us with all the traffic on the roads and the danger of accidents. But that's a commoner's life for you I suppose'.

Above Jack's farm the wooded heathland stretches away in sharp ridges and steep banks towards the coast. The Downs on the Isle of Wight form a blue band along the furthest horizon – a sure sign of rain to come according to the old farmer. The ground is carpeted in gold by last year's bracken. The gorse is in yellow flower. And small birds are beginning to make music as they sense the approach of spring. But this is wide, bleak country and not the place to come if you have a bad sense of direction or are timid in the wild: 'I don't find it lonely, but then I've lived in the place all my life, haven't I? To be honest, it can't be too quiet or too wild for me. I don't much look forward to the summer when the trippers come. And I've got my ponies out here for company too. That's the traditional Commoner's animal and they're all over the Forest. We take it for granted, but it's what the visitors come to see. One time I had about sixty-five of 'em out there. Keeping an eye on all of those kept me quite busy, I suppose. But since 1985 I've cut back to twenty-five horses. They all get branded come the autumn and each Commoner has his own individual brand so there aren't any mix-ups. What is different is that some animals do well on the poor Forest land and some don't do so well. Over the years different blood-lines have come in and the real New Forest ponies have been a bit diluted. The true ones will do fine out in the wild. The others may not do quite so well. One things that helps is that in March the Forestry do quite a bit of burning of the old bracken and gorse. Once you've burnt it off you always get a nice bit of growth come up afterwards. Six weeks later you see it all getting green and there's a good bit of bite for the cattle and the ponies then'.

One of Jack's first jobs in the morning is to go and call in his sheep from the meadow below the farm. The day is overcast and sullen but the ewes and their lambs are well wrapped against the cold. The old man trudges softly down the muddy track, stops at the battered iron gate and calls in his flock. They come running from far and wide bleating and crying and leaving white tufts of wool on the bramble bushes and the barbed wire fences: 'I haven't got so many sheep now. I've only got about thirty-five with their new lambs. But they make the fields good and clean, keeping down the ragwort and things like that. This year the lambing hasn't been too bad and we've got about one and a half per ewe on average. They're always pleased to see me in the morning, 'cos they've been waiting for their grub you see. They shout until they have their feed. Then they'll go off for the rest of the day and they'll be OK. They're like me. They're happy enough here. I shall never move from the Forest. It was where I was born and bred and I've known nothing different. I've been farming for meself here for close to fifty years and I don't suppose I've been away from the place about three weeks in all that time. I don't want to go anywhere for holidays. I've got all I want here. Trouble is, the modern people don't think like that. And that's why the old Commoners are dying out. You look around today and you see very few young chaps taking on the farming. And you can't blame them really because I don't think you can earn a living at it now. So I'm afraid that, in a hundred years time, there's unlikely to be people like me working in the New Forest. And it'll be the first time in a thousand years that there's not been'.

JUST to the north of Emery Down is a secret lake, hidden away in the depths of the Forest. Here, the Branscombe family, under the command of son Neil, run their Leominstead Trout Fishery. Visitors come from far and wide to try their luck on the black waters and to enjoy the wildlife and the surrounding scenery: 'On April days like this when it's more like January or February and the rain is pouring down from a sky as dark as the lake, you can't let up. You just have to get on with the job. It would be good if it was sunny and bright every day. But it's not and, if you have chosen an outdoor job you just have to put up with it. We have lads in the summer, they come down and see me sitting by the bank in the sunshine and think, 'Lovely job. I could do with some of that'. But they don't see it when it's like it is today when there's work that's got to be done and, like it or not, you've got to get out in the wet and roll your sleeves up. Some of the other ones, mind you – the die-hards they are – they come on down never mind the weather. They fish and we have a chat and that's good. It's a special lake – nothing artificial about it at all. It's about two hundred years old. It's meant to have been created by Capability Brown for the big estate here. The Manor House is just over the hill. They needed the lake for food. They used to grow carp in it I believe to feed the workers. So that's how it originated and then it's developed over the years into a trout fishery. I may sound knowledgeable about all this but I've had to learn it from scratch. I'm a boy from the Bush – Shepherds Bush in London. But I've seen the error of my ways

The Branscombe family run the Leominstead Trout Fishery. Pictured here with Neil are Old English Sheepdogs, Bruno and Beano.

and come down here. I've always fished, always had relations in the Forest. I suppose I got fed up with working in a factory. I was in the print trade and I'd had enough of it. Luckily enough me Dad wanted to do it too. He's a fisherman as well and we came down here together. We got the chance to buy this lake. We saw it advertised in the *Evening Standard* – not in *Sporting Life* or anything like that. So we took the chance and went for it. It's a wonderful place to work. A bit different from sodium lights and non-stop machinery. And I thoroughly enjoy it'.

Neil is a big man, strong and resolute, with tanned skin and spiky, black hair. A smile hovers around his mouth while he talks and his eyes are alert and intelligent. The rain lashes down and runs off his forehead and his cheeks. But he is well protected by waders and waterproofs. The surface of the lake is destroyed by the downpour and the surrounding trees sway with the onslaught. Many still show damage from the hurricane of 1987 and from the storms of January 1990. In spite of the wind a few hardy fishermen are still managing to cast their lines onto the lake. A couple of goodsized trout already lie dead on the shore beside the wooden pontoons: 'I suppose I've learnt quite a bit about fish in my time. How they feed and how they like to be treated. Right at the start I did some short courses just to learn a bit at the Hampshire College of Agriculture at Sparsholt. I got good basics there. A lot of the rest is just common sense really. You learn through experience how fish or any other animals are going to react. You make mistakes and you try and learn from them. You hope not to make too many because they can be costly. This time of the year – early spring – it's coming up to the beginning of the proper trout season. So what's important is that all the maintenance work is done so you've got a chance of a calm summer ahead of you. You shouldn't have too much heavy work to do during the fine months. You try to get most of that finished during the bad weather. The worst thing you can do when you've got a lot of people here out for a quiet day's fishing is to start crashing and bashing about and using a chain-saw and so on. Our customers come down here for a peaceful day by the water. They're miles from anywhere. There's no traffic noise. All they want is to have a happy day and to catch a few fish. Some jobs, of course, do have to be seen to. We stock the lake every day and that means netting the fish in the ponds and carrying them to the lake. We do that first thing usually. Then there's mending the wooden stages, which people fish from. They wear very quickly with the water and need doing regularly. Some of the fish want feeding too, so that's a daily job. One or two days a week we have deliveries coming in, so we have to net them from the tanks on the back of the truck, carry them to the ponds and make sure they're alright. Trout are curious creatures and they get very stressed up. The bigger the fish, the more worried they get. So you have to treat them very carefully. We have to look after the fishermen too sometimes. We had a lad come down once and, at lunch, he went down to the local ale-house. When he came back the landing-stage wasn't as long as he thought it was. So we had to haul him out. I don't know what the fish thought of that but, ever since then, he's been known as the guy who falls in the water after he's had a drink. Perhaps he hoped the lake was full of beer. Then, on the odd occasion, when a fish has hit the fly a chap has stepped back to strike and gone in. But it doesn't happen so often and round the stages the water's only waist deep and they just get a bit wet. We keep a few changes of dry clothes down here for these emergencies'.

As the skies begin to clear from the west, the day's consignment of trout arrives from Dorset in a battered pick-up truck. Among the hundreds of fish on board are three, fifteen pound monsters, which Neil will put in the lake at the start of the season to encourage his customers to come back often and try for one of the trout jackpots.

SWAN Green, just below Emery Down, is where Bob Murray makes his home. When he is not busy working all hours for the Electricity Board, Bob likes to walk in the New Forest watching deer and other wildlife. Sometimes on his travels he finds antlers which have been shed. Since 1964 he has been using them to make

At Swan Green, Bob Murray raises a hobby into an art form, making elegant walking sticks with antler handles.

elegant handles for the walking-sticks which he crafts in the workshop behind his home: 'Walking out in these old woods is my best relaxation. I can't think of anything nicer. I was born in the Forest and the only things that are free here are the air, the exercise and the views. But if I come across the odd antler out on the open heath I take it home with me. And I don't think anyone minds too much. My roots are deep in the place and I wouldn't want to do anything to harm it. I feel so lucky because I grew up here and live here still while most of the lads I went to school with don't even live within twenty miles. I enjoy watching the trees changing during the year, the woodland growing and spreading, the bird life, the deer, the badgers, rabbits and foxes. I also love the wind, the sun and even the rain. And I'm happy too in the shed behind my house working away at my walking-sticks. That all started getting on for thirty years ago and I'm a bit better at it now than I was then. At that time I became a member of the British Deer Society and started to go out looking for deer. Well, I needed a stick to make my way through the woods, so I made one for myself. To be honest, although I've still got it, I'm not too proud of it now. It's a bit rough and ready. But soon other people were asking me to make one for them. They used to give me little bits of antler to make into handles and then they'd bring me extra pieces too. So I built up a stock of it and had to find strong sticks to go with the horn – and it all grew from there. Word spread and I began to make them for people I'd never met. Now they've gone all over the world – to Egypt and Norway, Sweden, America, Germany and France'.

The small hut smells partly of a carpenter's, partly of a blacksmith's. Overall hangs the heady scent of strong glue. Piles of sticks are stacked in bundles on the rafters. Stacks of antlers of all sizes and colours are piled on the shelves. Tools lie scattered in intricate patterns. Bob bends over his vice, his eyes unblinking, as he makes the delicate join between wood and horn: 'You can only describe me as being self-taught. I have learnt, often through bitter experience, that there is a way to do each part of the process. First thing, I did it all wrong. I used copper tubing and there was glue and araldite all over the place. It was an awful mess. Now I've learnt to tidy things up a bit. I don't use any pipe at all and the antler is pinned to the stick with about five inches of metal studding with a thread running right the way through it. That takes the glue deep into the antler and into the stick and makes a really sound job. Another thing to learn about it is that it isn't a quick job. From the time you harvest the wood to when you finish the walking-stick takes nearly two years because the timber's got to season and dry out. Obviously, if you cut the wood at the wrong time, you'll get all sorts of problems with the bark. So you must always cut in the autumn or the winter so that the bark stays on the wood as it ought to. Of course, once I get into the workshop, I can put most sticks together in three or four hours from start to finish. That includes everything from dressing it down to fixing the antler onto the stock, finishing the horn off and then varnishing or polishing the stock, whichever the customer wants'.

Outside, an April shower drifts through the great Forest trees, which bend in the

H.H Munro or Saki had this advice in *The Square Egg* which he wrote in 1924: 'In baiting a mousetrap with cheese, always leave room for the mouse.' Even he would not have wished to catch this little fellow – a dormouse in his spring prime.

'There's a whisper down the field where the year has shot her yield,
And the ricks stand grey to the sun,
Singing: "Over then, come over, for the bee has quit the clover,
And your English summer's done" ' *Rudyard Kipling*

But even the most bored insect will not have ignored this lovely bee orchid with its seductive mirror image.

wind and the rain. Beside Bob's hut a fire, whipped up by the breeze, flames and crackles beneath a flat tub filled with warm, wet sand. Buried in the sand are the next sticks on which he will be working: 'Once the wood has been harvested, it's tied into bundles of between ten and twenty sticks each, nice and tightly, and stacked up in a corner of the shed after the first few months out of doors drying out slowly. Then, when they're ready to use, I light the fire underneath my steam box, which is full of sharp sand, which I've well dampened. Once it gets good and hot and the steam starts to come off, you bury the sticks in the sand for about ten or twelve minutes. Then what you have to do is to take each stick out in turn and straighten out any bends or kinks across your knee or through a hole in a piece of wood. I prefer to do it across my knee 'cos that way you don't damage or mark the bark. Once it's been straightened, it's stood in a corner and cools down and it will then stay exactly as you have made it, unless you're silly enough to leave it out in the rain when it will slowly go back to how it was before. But a straightened stick very rarely moves after it's been done. That's obviously provided that you harvest it correctly, store it properly and don't steam it too quickly. You need to let hazel weather for at least a year really and the harder woods for two years or more. Holly needs to wait seven years before you can use it and, if you're going to take the bark off it and reveal the lovely bone-like wood, you need to wait three or four years before you do that. If you take the bark off too early it will get what they call 'the shakes' and will split and not have a good finish at all. Once you've done all this and waited this long time, it's all systems go and you can't really afford to make any mistakes. The glue must be perfectly mixed, the holes drilled straight down the centre of the stick and the antler. You have to make everything just right in its final position, so you don't get any gaps or glue showing round the place where the stick joins the antler or the buffalo horn rings in between. The dowel, which holds the whole thing together, has to go perfectly straight and perpendicular into both the horn and the wood. If you get all these things right and a bit of luck as well, you'll end up with a walking-stick you can be proud of'.

DAVID Penny and Annette Booth live in Sleepy Hollow just opposite Emery Down Church. Both are keen horse-riders and David worked for twenty-five years at a local stud. Today, one of the few real foresters left in the village, he is the local handyman and gardener in some of the fine houses in the area: 'I reckon I know this place quite well by now, seeing I've been living about here for fifty years, even a bit more than that. Went to school here in the old village school. Was born and lived at the farm where my family is still working. I've poached rabbits out of most of the hedges and burrows. Done just about everything you can do in a place like this. And I think it's a good life as you can have here in the New Forest. For work, I do anything that comes along. Now and again the phone rings and the voice says, 'Dave, could you come and help'. Same with Annette – she gets jobs just the same way. It might be delivering foals or calves. Could be a bit of plumbing, fencing or mending. Sometimes it's gardening – just about anything I can turn my hand to. Sometimes it's a success, sometimes it's not. I picked up everything I know from my family I suppose. There's quite a lot of Pennys hereabouts. It was ten boys and two girls in our family. We lost one boy about five years ago, but the rest are still alive. And I think there's about ninety nieces and nephews and great-nieces and grand-nephews. I can't keep up with them all to tell you the truth. They come along and say, 'Hello uncle' and I say to them, 'Which one are you then?' That's a good New Forest family I suppose. Some people would agree with that and some wouldn't. And there are a few others like it round here – the Witchers, the Gaylers and the Waghorns – all good Forest people. But nowadays we've got an invasion of what they call yuppies, who, unfortunately, want to run the place. As soon as they arrive they want to change everything; they have to put extensions on here, new bit on there, tell everyone how to carry on. Sad fact is that I've lived here fifty-five years now and I think there's only eight of us left now – original people'.

The face is weathered and weary and lined from a thousand storms. The words follow one another swiftly with an expectant chuckle at the end of the sentences. The eyes are bright and inquisitive and there is a challenge in them to strangers or to impertinent questions: 'It may sound strange but I've never wanted to go anywhere else, I was in the Army for a bit, went abroad and loved it out there. But I still couldn't get back here fast enough. We've still got the two old ponies. No dog any more, but I walk other people's for them and enjoy doing that. I don't think I'll move now. Don't reckon I've got many more years, do you? Not many more chocolates left in the box they reckon. But still plenty to do to keep me busy. Today, for instance, I've got to take down the notice-board outside the Church. Annette does some jobs for the Rear-Admiral who lives up at Bank and he asked her to get me to take the sign down 'cos it wants re-paintin'. That was about a fortnight ago and she's got to go back there to work tomorrow and he'll want to know why it haven't been taken down. So got to get to it. It's been up there a few years now – and so has the vicar. After that I've got to get the old Ferguson tractor out and cart some manure with it. It's nearly fifty years old. Annette found it under a holly bush out at Salisbury. We got it carted 'ome and a chap did the job on it. She started up fine and went for about three months. Then all of a sudden it stopped. We couldn't find out what was wrong. So I got my nephew to have a look at it and he found she had so much water in her he thought she was a steam engine. He didn't think it could ever have worked. But he's redone it and away she goes. Apart from the manure, we bring our wood back from the Forest with her. And what we don't bring back on the tractor we fetch home by hand when we're taking the dogs out. If you carry a couple of sticks back each night with you, that keeps the fire going all winter. Never come back empty-'anded. All my life I've done things like that. I remember so well the old days when I used to walk up from the farm to school. Sometimes we took with us our four-wheeled trolleys and we used to go all down the road and never saw anybody – not a soul. Sometimes we'd pass old Mr White and his baker's cart. That's the only chap we ever met, I think. Or perhaps an old International van used to plod round the corner, driven by old Dusty Miller from up Silver Street, who just died not long ago. He used to give us a lift sometimes and we was thrilled to bits. Or Mr Payne, who was the undertaker and builder – he's gone now too. He'd always give us a ride in his horse and cart or on the old lorry he used to drive. Spite of all that I was always late for school anyway 'cos I was up a tree somewhere or up to some mischief. I got the cane more times than enough. I even had a big hat with 'D' on it put on my head once and was made to stand in the corner. And I doubt I've made much progress ever since'.

SOME of the best bulls in the land are quartered on the outskirts of Lyndhurst, just across the Forest from Emery Down. This is the Hampshire Cattle Breeders' AI centre and the stockman in charge of these magnificent animals is Tony Vellam, who has been in the job for over thirty years. His father and grandfather were both herdsmen, but neither of them can have imagined the splendour of the beasts for which Tony is responsible: 'One of the kindest and quietest bulls here is a Hereford. He's got no horns, which the old Hereford breeders wouldn't have thought much of. They used to all be horned you see but over the years we've bred them out. The advantages of having them hornless are obvious. When you've got a bunch of steers or heifers or cows together there's a lot of damage can be done by horned heads. With bulls the most important thing is that they must have good legs and feet. As a matter of fact I think that's the vital thing with all livestock. But with a beef bull you've got to try and look at it from the butcher's point of view. He wants meat all the way through right from the shoulder all the way to the hindquarters. There's nothing much use on the head nor on the legs so what he wants is a blocky looking bull – like a brick with the legs on the four corners. For me personally, I like to see large beef animals. They've tended to get bigger over the years and I think it's been a great improvement, especially with the Herefords. The bad side of the job for me is when they get too old to do their job here and have to go off to the butcher. I hate to see that. We've had one old Hereford here, a horned one, that was with us for ten years. It did grieve me to see him go. His name wouldn't mean anything to you but that old bull sired forty thousand calves in Hampshire while he was with us in the stud'.

The sound of the bulls in the AI centre at feeding time is like the noise in the lion house at the London Zoo. It is a mixture of snarling, groaning, bellowing and whining and drowns out the roar of the traffic on the Brockenhurst road. Clouds of rooks and starlings, scared by the male chorus, scatter in the overcast afternoon sky as Tony and his team wheel barrows of food along the aisles and fill basins and troughs for their hungry charges: 'They take a lot of looking after, though not as much as cows do. The difficulty is in their nature. They're aggressive and, if you're handling them, you need more people to do it. They weigh about a ton each and you don't want to fool around with anything as heavy and as fierce as that. Some of them are untrustworthy. Some don't trust you. Some have no fear at all of human beings. But, in the main, with a stud of fifty bulls like this, you're likely to get a mixture. They're not all going to be evil or wicked bulls that are waiting for an opportunity to get you. You're also certain to find ones with a kindly disposition and which are quite placid. Curiously, the beef bulls have the best temperament. It's usually with the dairy bulls that you find some that would have a go at you. It's an old saying but the important thing is to treat them with respect. It's not just their temper. It's because they're so massive and through their sheer size, they could do you some damage just by leaning against you. I've been with livestock all my life you see. Since I was eleven years old I helped my father to milk the cows. He kept bulls of course because those were the early days before AI had really taken up. So I got used to them then and I suppose it's been my life really. Perhaps cattle are part of my heritage. One thing I know is how much good the bull stud here has done for the New Forest. If you think of the old times when every little farmer had some raggedy old bull. Now they have access to some of the best there are in the business. There used to be a lot of fertility and disease problems in the Forest cattle and the existence of this place has improved the small Forest herds out of all recognition. For me, the pleasure of the job is just starting with May approaching. Soon the bulls will be out to grass, once there's a good growth on the meadow. It's wonderful to see them tethered there on a summer evening. When they've had a good drink of water after a hot day, I can look out of my dining-room window and see them out there chewing the cud or eating the grass and it's a very satisfying sight. It makes my life worthwhile'.

IT is pleasantly typical of England that somewhere which has been in existence for close to a thousand years should still be called The New Forest. It was christened originally by William the Conqueror to contrast it with Savernake Forest, which had, even at that time, been a Royal Forest of the chase for more than a century. Isolated places like Emery Down have dotted its heathland across the centuries, though their inhabitants are mostly rather better heeled today than they were in the past. What has not changed over the years is the feeling of remoteness and timelessness in its wild woodland and on its rolling plains. Here, Foresters long dead would still feel themselves at home and would be able to thread their way through the gorse and along the old tracks, which so bamboozle today's timid tourists. Perhaps some of the intricacies of Alice in Wonderland's story come from these woodland glades. The girl on whom Alice was based lived near Emery Down and lies buried in Lyndhurst churchyard. Much has changed since her day but much, thank heaven, still remains the same.

THE FOREST OF BERE

THERE was a time when the countryside between Southampton and Portsmouth was threatened by talk of a Solent City with concrete and tower blocks abounding. And indeed, if you travel the coast road between the two cities, you can scarcely find a hundred yard stretch which remains undeveloped. But to the north of the M27 is a patch of the best of Hampshire surrounding the villages of Southwick, Wickham, the Boarhunts, Denmead, Soberton Heath and Hambledon, where cricket was born. This is the ancient Forest of Bere, which once stretched from Kings Somborne on the river Test eastwards through Eastleigh and Bishops Waltham – a great swathe of heath and woodland nearly eight miles wide.

The word 'bere' is said to describe the pastures in the forest. But some locals swear that it means bears of the furry and clawed variety. Perhaps that great diarist Samuel Pepys had this in mind when he travelled to Portsmouth Dockyard in 1662. He wrote; 'Up early in Petersfield and thence got a countryman to guide us to Havant to avoid going through the Forest.'

It would be a surprise to encounter a bear today in this golden part of Hampshire. But in June you will enjoy the Southern English countryside at its summery best and most beautiful.

DEEP inside the Forest of Bere Ken Galton from Southwick regularly collects wood from an old coppice. Years ago as a child he learnt to make hurdles from a man whose family had been doing the intricate job for generations. The work is hard, heavy and unrelenting and the rewards are small. But Ken would not swap his skills and he is determined to pass them on to the next generation so that the numbers of craftsmen will not be further reduced: 'When I first started in the 1950s there was a matter of fifty 'urdle-makers in the Lockerley and Kings Somborne area. Now you can just count 'em on one 'and. And there's not so much wood for us now neither because so much has been cleared through farming. In the late '50s and early '60s a lot of pine plantations were put in to the ground we'd cleared of hazel-wood or chestnut for our 'urdles. So we're gradually pushed farther and farther out. But I'm not giving in yet. I always remember as a boy going off in the 'orse and cart to the woods picking up 'urdles. Then bringing 'em back and putting them on the train. That was before I started making 'em. I was just a youngster. But I suppose I got the taste for it then.'

The eyes are sharp and clear and the body thin and muscled. There is great economy of movement as the strong, scarred hands twist and bend, chop and slice, split and point the young wood. A lifetime of experience goes into every phase of the work: 'In spite of the difficulties and the bad weather, the travelling to the

Ken Galton from Southwick keeps alive the ancient craft of hurdle making, deep in the Forest of Bere.

woods and the traffic I still get a lot of satisfaction out of the job. Most of all I get it when I'm deep in the woods and its quiet and I'm on my own. Sometimes people say it's dangerous in case you have an accident. And I did once. I cut a tendon on my thumb. We always used billhooks them days. And a glancing blow come up and cut me. That was after I'd been doing it for about eleven years. So it's not too bad – one little accident after nearly forty years in the business. I was always out in the woods as a boy round the hurdle-makers and all the others too. So when I left school me brother was doing it already and I took it up. The old chap that was doing it then, he taught me. He'd been doing it all his life and 'is father before him. So he had plenty of experience to pass on and to help me on my way.'

The strong wooden barrier grows slowly as Ken moves methodically back and forth. Each piece of wood binds itself to its neighbour and the thin strips thread their way through the uprights. It seems a miracle that they do not break when they are forced reluctantly through some of the narrow gaps: 'There's more to it than anybody thinks by just watching you doing it. I've let people have a go before now and then they realise what skill there is. You need to watch someone who don't know how having a go. And there are a few folk about trying to make

42

'urdles for a living, who have half picked it up or thinks they knows how to do it and don't. But of course it's not a good product they make. And it spoils the trade. Them 'urdles fall to pieces cause they're not built on a curve. As they dry out they straighten up and tighten up, and soon they get all loose and start falling to pieces. The 'ardest things to learn about the job is splitting the wood and twisting it. With both of them it's a matter of going off and practising. You have to get the right pressures. Nowadays I can split them down by feel and I've no need to look at what I'm doing. I know which way the split's doing, whether it's running out to the left or the right. It looks easy enough but it's not. And it's not simple finding the wood either. I'm looking for young hazel-wood – seven to eight years old. I get through about three acres a year. If I could find more I could be teaching a lad to do it like I was once taught. But I'm travelling about sixty-four mile round trip to gather up wood, so there's no time or money for that. It all adds up to the fact that I doubt there'll be any one much doing this job fifty years from now. And that's sad. But with the scarcity of coppices and the high price of local cottages it'll just become impossible. And it's a fine type of work. Nothing better really. You've got all your animals and birds around you and plenty to see and enjoy. It's a bit lonely at times and you can get fed up with things if it's wet or cold or if something goes wrong. But I've got through it the last forty years, so I think I'll get over a few more yet.'

As the wood is tamed and tied into bundles two collar doves exchange kisses in the tree above and a wren scolds a trespassing neighbour from the thicket. They seem to count the woodman as one of their own number, and to accept him gladly.

ERNIE Tee's family has lived in the Forest of Bere for over four centuries. Today, he and his wife exist in a way which their ancestors would still recognise. They milk their own cows, sell eggs and grow vegetables. Ernie started milking by hand 74 years ago and he looks with some sadness on the world that has grown up around him since those distant days: 'Haven't been nowhere else. Born in Denmead and never been out and I don't intend to go neither. I don't want to go out of Denmead for anyone. Trouble is, it's all outsiders here now and that's what's finished it. Them days we had to work but we never grumbled. Fact is, I loved it. I'd do anything to stay 'ome from school to work – anything to get out of school. Many a time, when I was eight or nine years old, I was told we've got some jobs to do today and you've got to stop home from school. Suited me. I didn't want no school. No schoolmaster never used to bother about us. We just got on with it. And the old vicar used to come around every week and say to us, 'Sons of the soil you are and that's what we want'. Didn't bother about anyone else. Didn't wan't to change nothing. Then, for several of us, if we'd been to school and came home nights it was straight to work on the farm till the jobs was done. Father left school when he was eleven. Mother too. And I left at fourteen. And it didn't 'urt 'em, did it? They had to work all their lives and mother went on into her nineties. And they did as well and better than folks with a lot of learnin'.'

The old man walks slowly to the meadow in the early sunshine to call in the cows. He scratches his head under a battered hat and the creased face softens as he looks out over the valley. The sounds of the farmyard surround him: 'Before leaving for school we had to get the cows in first and help milk. Then, on the way to school, we drove the cows up in the field close by, so we could bring 'em home again at night. Next we had the morning's wood to get 'cos there was no gas nor electric. Chop the wood for the fire and light it up for our early cup of tea. So it was up early and off. When we was 'aymaking we'd be up at four o'clock in the morning and go grass-cutting with the 'orses. It wasn't much of a living then – not now neither – but we'd get by. We all 'elped one another. We always 'ad a pig indoors look. And always had plenty of bacon, and always had some chickens. Father used to go and kill the pigs for all the neighbours round here, 'cos all the cottages 'ad a great big one. So they'd bring her in and father would kill 'un and then at night he'd cut it up for them – and it lasted them a year. It was half-a-crown to kill the pig and one-and-sixpence to cut 'em up. And if they had two killed at once – the grocer and the baker for instance – it was only two shillings each to kill. Thursday night it was – he always killed on the Thursday. Old Charlie Pratt, he used to come in and buy the fat. Fat pork – just pure fat as thick as your arm. Put it in a pan he did and he'd say: 'Well we shall be all right now. That'll last me all the winter.' And that's how they used to go on. Never hurt them did it?'

The small thatched house lies half buried by trees and bushes. Cats and dogs, hens and cockerels, sparrows galore pick their way round the debris of the years of self-sufficiency. They come crowding eagerly around when Ernie emerges to throw them some corn: 'Them old days we used to sell eggs too. Before I left school I 'ad to go down to me uncle who had a food round in Portsmouth. Had to take the 'orse and van every Friday and bring butter and eggs. And pigs too if there was any. Used to go every Friday rain, hail or shine. And it wasn't a very pleasant job because when we used to come back home in the winter we couldn't see much at all. We used to have an old candle on the van. Never even lit up the 'orse's tail let alone the road ahead. It was black dark coming through those woods at South-wick. Anyway, my uncle would put a pound of butter and half-a-dozen eggs all nicely in a basket and take it down to an old lady who lived in a great big house in Southsea. She was rich all right. But she'd ask how much. Two shillings a pound for butter and two shillings for a dozen eggs. 'It's too much,' she's say, 'don't you come no more with any eggs till they're one and six.' So that's what we had to accept. Used to go down every bloomin' Friday. I detested it. Had to walk all up Portsdown Hill, then drive down the other side. When you come back you 'ad the walk all the way up from the Alexandra Hospital all up over the hill to get home again. No matter what the weather or the season, you still 'ad to go – winter or summer. Don't want no more of it now.'

44

Ernie Tee farms in the same traditional way as his family before him, stretching back over four centuries in Denmead.

While the early sun streaks the barn floor and cats and kittens queue up for a warm drink, Ernie presses his head against the flank of his brown and white house cow and milks steadily. Every now and again he pauses to tip some into the tin pan beneath his battered chair, where the cats squabble and shove like supermarket shoppers: 'Done this ever since I was seven, so it shouldn't seem like hard work now should it? If I've done it for seventy years I can do it on automatic now and if I don't know how to milk a cow by this time I never shall. When I was too small to do it, Mother used to milk 'em – twice a day and every day. Father was out with the horses and that. Didn't seem to have much time 'cos he used to have to go down to Portsmouth with loads of faggots or hay. The wood was for the bake-houses. They used to put the wood in the ovens, burn it till it was ashes, then put the bread in. And weren't those buns nice when they came out 'ot. A ha'penny each! Good for your health too. That's why I think I've got a few years yet. 'Ope I can go to a hundred. I shall keep going if I can. I won't give in. You know, one of my uncles went to 97. And an old great-aunt went to 99. Told me father she didn't want to get to a hundred. Said, 'I only want to live to 99'. She died on her 99th birthday. So that was good going, wasn't it?'

The old man stretches his arms and unties the cow, so that she can wander back to her summer meadow. The cats and kittens lie sleeping in a contented bundle. Ernie heads for the yard and the ducks, which are clamouring to be fed.

In her narrow back garden at Soberton Heath, Rosemary Webb looks after more than twenty classy Shetland ponies. It is no surprise that her house is a magnet for local youngsters, who come to help and to ride – until they get too large for the tiny animals. These ponies have been shown at Olympia and throughout the country and they proudly carry with them a little bit of Hampshire wherever they go: 'This all started because I've got a Welsh Cob, who's 29 now and was in the field next door. I bought the first two Shetlands as companions for him. The truth is that I bought one. But then, because the big horse comes into the stable at night, I thought the Shetland would be lonely in the field. So I got another one to keep him company. Then gradually I got more and, as I became interested in showing, I built it up to six. And, because everything I buy I keep, it just grew and grew. Next I thought that I should start running a little riding school, since I had taught riding before anyway. Then I wanted to get better ponies without wanting to lose the others. And so it went on. I think I ought to warn people that if ever they buy a Shetland as a companion they should think about it very carefully because it never ends. They really get hold of you.'

Rosemary's back garden is a modern version of the Biblical camel and the eye of the needle. There are ponies everywhere. And where there are no ponies there are sheds full of harness and hay and sacks of feed. And where there are no sheds there are dunghills. And where there are no dunghills there are hordes of scampering girls: 'A few people in the village are very kind and, when they've got a little bit of land, they let me have it and we use that for a few weeks till the grass has gone. But the show ponies have to be stabled because they're in and out all the time working hard and it's easier to keep them in show condition if they're kept in at night. Usually my neighbours are very tolerant because they have to put up with quite a lot. Luckily, on one side, they've got several dogs, so it's all animals together. On the other side they've got a beautiful garden. But so far we've had no disasters and we try not to make ourselves a nuisance to them.'

An unending string of small girls on stubby ponies winds its way through the Webbs' garden gate and away down the road. Mothers walk beside the youngest girls and push them upright if they begin to slide. Soon they reach a meadow full of pygmy jumps and obstacles and begin to practise under Rosemary's vigilant supervision: 'This is where we come to do all our training – flat riding, jumping, gymkhana work, pony-handling. What we do depends on the age and ability of the child. At the moment we're rehearsing like mad for the Shetland Society's Centenary. From all over the country – from the north of Scotland to the South Coast – we've put together a musical ride, which we do at the Royal Highland Show, the Royal Show in Warwickshire and all over the place. That's for the bigger girls, of course. For the little ones we go out hacking down our disused railway line, which is just down the road. We take them out for three-quarters of an hour mostly on the leading rein. And it makes a beautiful ride through the woods. Another excitement we've had was the Queen Mother's ninetieth birthday celebrations in London. The Shetland Society was asked to present a little tableau in the march past. It was of a lead-rein pony in hand, two riding ponies and a pair of driven ponies. One of mine, Trampers, was chosen to represent the Society and it was absolutely wonderful. I'm still high about it today. But when all that's said and done, I still wouldn't want to come home to anywhere but here. I still love it as much as the day I came out – twenty years ago now. And when I go to Portsmouth to see my mother and my aunt and when I'm heading back over Portsdown Hill I look at the scene ahead of me and the Forest of Bere and it's like coming home in the very best sense of the word. I think myself lucky every time I'm able to do it.'

Along the old railway line the chatter of little voices and the clatter of small hooves fade into the distance. The woodland regains its composure and a cock pheasant calls crossly from the thicket.

DAVE Cox used to walk past the old forge in Denmead on his way to school each day. Now he runs the smithy in Southwick and the metal creations which he has made there have won him prizes at many local shows. His jam comes from the forging of works of art out of red-hot iron. But his bread and butter remains the daily slog of repairing and welding farm machinery: 'We go all over the place and every day is totally different. We do metal work anywhere any time. Quite a lot for the Council and the Forestry Commission, for farmers, schools – all that kind of thing. I go out into the Forest of Bere quite a bit – welding machinery that's broken down and other work on site. You have to be mobile because it's impossible for some of the things to be brought here to the forge. The Denmead blacksmith was called Mr Tee when I was a youngster there. And I used to look over the stable door on my way to school and the fire would be blazing and the sparks flying. It was every schoolboy's dream I suppose and all I ever wanted to do was to get into blacksmithying. Well, when I left school, I had the devil of a job getting into it because they all said that it was a dying trade. But I persevered and in the end I got in, and I've been doing it now for eighteen years. We had a bunch of kids in from a school the other day. It reminded me of when I was their age. And one little lad wanted to know how I had started and whether I'd learnt it from my father. He was really surprised to hear that neither my mother nor my father was a blacksmith. He seemed to think it quite possible that a woman could do the job.'

Out in a fire-break in the forest Dave arrives with his is mobile forge to work on a huge tractor, which is in need of some expert welding. A torrent of sparks fly onto the leather apron and bounce down onto the earth. Tall trees shade the sun but the ruddy face sweats with the weight and the heat of the work: 'It's a hard trade all right, but not a dying one I don't think. The only thing that would kill it might be the people around who take short cuts. Too many of them, I'm afraid and their work's not up to scratch. The forge really is the only way to do any form of serious ironwork – and it's important to stick to it. I've had my moments too though when everything's not gone perfectly. Quite a lot of the time I'm off demonstrating at Agricultural or Craft Shows. Lots of people stand round and watch you. I normally avoid drinking on these occasions – mainly because I don't like buying it. But one day someone came over with a pint of beer and, being fairly hot with the work and the sun, I drank it down quickly. Well, it went straight to my head. I suppose it was partly because I hadn't eaten. So I picked up the hammer to carry on forging and bringing it up to strike the metal the head of the hammer hit me right up on the side of my nose. The people who were watching were quite surprised to see a blacksmith working away with the tears running down his face.'

The forge at Southwick sits below the village and has an interior as dark as a cave. It is sooty black inside and the rafters are caked with dirt and dust. All around, in organised confusion, are the tools of the blacksmith's trade. As he concentrates on his work between the anvil and the blazing coals, Dave's face shines with sweat in the golden light: 'I'm fairly big anyway, but you do need strength for the job. There's no doubt of that. But, when you come down to the sculptures that I do, they're very light. And I get more enjoyment out of them than I do out of the big stuff. The challenge with working with small pieces is that you've got to be very quick with them. It's a matter of timing more than anything. If you've got something in the fire, you've got this built-in clock that tells you when to take it out. So the timing is vital and, I suppose, having a good eye too. That all comes from experience, of course. Because you go on learning every day. Every piece you work on has something to tell you and it never goes quite the same as the one before. So you're making mental notes all the time. You need dedication too. You've got to be committed to your work. And you need to know about metal – what you can do with it and what you can't. One of my specialities is a ram's head. I like the way it looks with its great, curling horns. One of its virtues is that you can make it from start to finish in about twenty minutes. So, at the shows, the visitors – and particularly the children – can stand and watch something being completed. The other thing I do is trees. They came about mainly because of Dutch Elm Disease destroying so many of those beautiful great giants. All around there were these dark, twisted silhouettes, which I've tried to copy in metal. The silly thing is that I don't much like to sell them after I've made them because they mean so much to me still. The work in the forge I love. It's a big part of my life. But I'm lucky to be able to go out and work in these lovely woods too. You're completely isolated out there and you feel useful because someone's broken down and desperately needs the skills I've learnt to get them going again. There's true satisfaction in that.'

At the top of the village, through the quiet summer air, you can hear the ringing of the anvil half a mile away as bright and cheerful as the song-birds in the hedges along the allotments.

FOREST Farm lies close to Denmead and houses a family race-horse stable owned and master-minded by Michael Madgewick, who rides, trains, manages and shares the work with his team. The stables cater for some twenty horses and every day they stretch their legs on the gallops close beside the woodland of the Forest of Bere: 'This was a pig farm when we first come here. Didn't look much like it does now, of course. Well, we'd always had 'orses and the pig job wasn't very good at that time. So I decided to go all to 'orses. The big thing was getting people to think that you could do a job for them. And the first one who sent me an 'orse to train was Tony Grantham, who was a National Hunt jockey. Well that 'orse won. So he sent me another one and that came in first too with his son riding it. So the word got around and things just moved on from there. You don't advertise for owners to come to you. It's just people say, 'Oh Michael Madgewick, he's not doing a bad job. You know, I think I'll send him a horse.' And they do and, even if they're at the bottom end of the market, which they often are, you still do the best you can with 'em. Sometimes they might have leg trouble and you try to patch 'em up. Or maybe they'll be unbroken. And that's best of all because, if it learns any bad habits or makes mistakes, that's your fault. But, if it gets it right, that's your responsibility too and you can take pride in that.'

In the early morning the stable yard is bustling with preparations. Horses are being groomed and saddled while others look enviously on. Stable lads and jockeys exchange sly jokes and sparrows scream self-importantly from the rafters. There is no cavalry twill or thousand pound binoculars at this yard. Everything is practical and done for a purpose: 'At the moment we've got nine flat horses here. And so far this season we've managed to win four races. Believe it or not, I had a day at Ascot for the first time, dressed up with the top hat and the tails. And he run well – the horse ran well. He won a race at Brighton a week before Ascot and the owner decided he'd like to take him to the big races. He asked me what I thought and I said, 'Well, you know, it's up to you. It's your horse. You pay the bills.' So I entered him and he went there. And he was a 100-1 outsider and he finished seventh or eighth. I was highly delighted and excited too because he was well up there for a lot of the race. But I'm back down to earth now and into the regular routine. It's the same thing every morning really. Up early and the lads tack up. They make their way down through the forest to where the gallop is. And that's a grand hack. It's a lovely walk down that road – a bit of traffic may be – but the horses enjoy it and so do we. I know they're enjoying it because they're all running well. Then when they get to the gallop they give 'em a canter. They don't actually gallop them flat out or nothing like that. The thing is just to keep 'em fit, keep 'em happy. Then back they come, wash 'em off and back in the stables. And that's the routine every day for us. We thrive on it and so do the horses'.

TRAVELLING through these Hampshire lanes, it is hard to imagine this area covered by primeval forest. And yet, with the oaks and the beeches thick with their summer leaves, you can round a corner and still feel shut in by woodland on every side. If you stand on a hill and look around you it is pleasantly possible to feel surprised at the number of trees which remain – traces of the wild, old Forest of Bere in this most cultivated and prosperous of counties. When we find ourselves tempted to criticise people in distant lands for cutting down or burning their forests, it is worth remembering that our ancestors have done exactly the same over the centuries. If they had not done so, the English landscape, which we know and love today, would not exist.

THE NADDER VALLEY

THE River Nadder winds lazily through Wiltshire from Donhead St Andrew to its meeting with the Avon at Salisbury. Its name has only a coincidental connection with snakes – Nydd is the Celtic word to twist or bend and Dwr is the name for water. Hence Nydd-Dwr – today Nadder. And there is hardly a straight reach in the whole river's length. The countryside which surrounds it is some of the best which Wiltshire can put on display – softly wooded down, rich cornfields, small thatched villages, welcoming pubs and people who are proud of their patch. In the high summer this is country flowing with milk and honey – and corn. Much of the harvest is already safely gathered in and the land lies silent, resting and awaiting the coming of the plough. Birds and beasts shelter from the heat and keep their silence. Only human beings go about their business along either side of the gentle stream.

HIGH above the small town of Tisbury, which got its name 1200 years ago from the teasles which were then used for cloth-making, Arthur Lushe, still young at heart in his retirement, tends his immaculate garden and works steadily in the August sunshine. Once he worked for the RAF at nearby Chilmark, but now he has time to take things more easily, to remember and to relax: 'I was born here in 1919 and have lived here off and on ever since. I've wandered a bit in this country and in the Far East during the war years. But I decided to come back here and settle down and, I hope, to enjoy my retirement and do more of the things that I'd always wanted to do and have time to do them. There's everything I want here. It just falls in line with my way of life – to be peaceful and quiet and to have the countryside close by. Then, if I want to go anywhere, I can take the train because we're one of those lucky villages nowadays which still has a railway station. So I can go almost anywhere quite easily. But usually I like to stay put. That's in spite of the changes here. Because – not wanting to knock them – the village has mainly come into the possession of money people now. They're rich and they've bought the best houses and that means the local people have no chance at all of getting properties round here. And little by little the village has altered. I can remember when I knew eighty percent of the people who lived here. Now I doubt I know twenty percent. Because it's all strangers from other parts of the country who like to come here, no doubt for the same reasons as I do, in search of a bit of peace and quiet after the rough and tumble of their lives. And that of course does change the face of the village because, instead of villagers, we have so many outsiders. Some of them come here with revolutionary ideas and get onto committees and say that they're going to do goodness knows what. That's until it comes to doing something about it and then you don't see them any more. Some of the ideas are good too, but carrying them out is the problem'.

The hoe clinks against the pebbles as Arthur attacks the weeds in his colour-filled garden. His wife walks steady journeys with a big watering-can refreshing the thirsty flowers and vegetables. The sun stands directly overhead and widens the cracks in the parched earth. It has been a drought summer of foreign intensity but the beds are full of healthy plants in rich variety: 'I'll be honest with you, I hate gardening. I do it under sufferance. Having said that, I'm still glad I've got it because, if I need to, I can always escape out here. When I've had enough of the indoor life and things aren't going too good I think, 'Right, I'll bugger off down the garden now'. And then when I get out here I manage to find it really interesting – even though I moan about it and say that I wish I didn't have it. It's worthwhile because all the plants I have I grow from seeds and then bring them into the borders and the beds – that's the vegetable line and the flower line too. I find that a real challenge. And I'm proud of my tools as well. Now my hoe was made by a blacksmith that used to work at a little village near here called Teffont. He was a farmer too and good at his job. He used to be clever enough to make those beautiful wrought-iron gates that you sometimes see with roses and petals and those kind of things on them. He could talk away while he worked, even on those complicated things, 'cos he was a proper character and liked nothing better than for people to go and chat to him. But he wouldn't stop working 'cos he reckoned no work, no money. All the time he was nattering away he'd have his old anvil there and he'd be hammering away and searing with bits of metal flying every-where. It used to fascinate me watching him. Now sometimes he used to do odd jobs and, if you were on the right side of him, you could go down and say, 'Harry, will you make me a hoe?' And he'd say, 'Of course I'll make you a hoe, me son'. So, having pestered him for long enough, one day he set about it. He picks up the bits of metal from his scrap-heap and taps them against one another, which was the way the old smiths used to assess the quality of the steel they were going to use. After a bit he said, 'That'll do'. Well, the blade of it is a piece of an old scythe, which is what they used to cut the corn crops with many years ago. The frame was made out of all sorts of bits of old iron which went into the forge and were bent to the shapes which he'd chosen. And when he'd finished it he said, 'There y'are me old son. There's your 'oe. Now don't keep on at me any more. He'll last you yer lifetime, so don't come back for another'. And to this day that hoe has given me very good service. In actual fact it's as good now as it was the day he made it. And that's after forty years of use, which speaks for itself. I've no doubt that he was right and that it will see me out. As I've grown older, I've found that the hoeing and the digging is getting harder – even with the old hoe. My garden is fifty yards long and I've got the two plots. At the start of the season it's a bit frightening when you think that you've got all that digging to do. I've been labouring away at it all these years and never turned up anything worth finding in the way of coins or

A perfect summer day beside the river Frome at Wool in deepest Dorset. Here Thomas Hardy dreamt his dreams and wove his magic. Here even the weariest wanderer can find peace in the heart of the forgotten county.

Badgers are bold and brave, inquisitive and strong. They have as many friends as they have enemies. But they are also cautious and shy and are only seen by the very patient or the very lucky.

valuables. See the same old soil again and again and know where it's stony and where it's not stony. But the only thing to do is to get out there and just keep digging and hope that you're going to feel the hedge at the bottom tickling the back of your neck and then you think, 'Oh, thank God, I've got there'. And that's how I go on. I couldn't possibly dig it all in one go, but however long it takes I'm very glad indeed when I've got to the end of it'.

On a placid stretch of the Nadder, shaded by a weeping willow, Arthur Lushe stands looking at the river in the breathless, August heat. Rod in hand he watches his float on the surface of the languid, black water. He is a chubby, cheerful man with good-natured lines round his eyes and mouth. Even when he is intent on his fishing he still seems to be smiling. On his head is a Mr Toad cap with the slimmest of peaks. Below it the eyes observe and calculate and the hands gently pull in the line: 'I've fished this river off and on for fifty years or more. It used to be much better for fishing than it is now. Once it was stocked and looked after by the Estate and there was a good variety of fish in it. Then they decided to develop it for trout only and that did harm because they persecuted all the coarse fish. Their theory was that they ate the trouts' food though that's open to dispute. The poor, old pike was attacked for getting after the trout. But you can argue about that too, because he's a scavenger and he's not going to chase about after really fit fish if there's some sick and ailing ones in the river and some rough, old things creeping about. So even the pike has a purpose and perhaps taking out the amount they did was not a good thing for the fishing, because you end up with all sorts of fish that, if Nature had her way, would not be alive. Anyway, the water is owned by a farmer now and is rented to Tisbury Angling Club, of which I'm a founder member. There was half-a-dozen of us got together one day, many years ago and formed the Club. What's hurt it today is the competition fishing. People who do this to get trophies and prizes and to make money out of it are not fishermen. Fishing is a sport and should be treated like one. I still come down here though for a bit of relaxation. None of your dry fly or wet fly for me. I'm a simple man and I'm after the old carp and other coarse fish with paste bait and breadcrust. Nothing too fancy. I also use worms and they're as good as anything at this time of year because, although we had a summer storm the other day, the water is quite placid and the river's running deep and slow. In those conditions worm is quite tempting and easily seen by the flesh-eating fish. My theory about fishing is quite an obvious one really. It is that nothing's going to eat if it isn't hungry. We don't – not many of us anyway – and nor do they. And I think with pike in particular, which I used to go for, they definitely have set feeding times and so there are periods in the day when it's much better to go fishing for them than other times. My trouble this morning – and the reason I'm not doing too well – is that the worms have been in captivity for some while. During this hot weather they tend to get laggy. I keep them in moss because they say that it hardens the outer skin, which makes it easier to put on the hook but I sometimes wonder if it makes it less exciting for the fish to eat. Because they're very fussy things, fish. They're a bit like us in that way. They seem to like best of all flat-tailed worms called lob-worms. There are too many types of worms for me to know all the names, but that is their favourite down here on the Nadder. It's a reddish worm with a flat tail and doesn't grow to a great size'.

Before long the heat persuades Arthur that he and the fish have had enough. So as usual, when he is in the mood, he heads for the Crown Inn opposite Tisbury Church to chat with his friends, to enjoy a pint or two and sometimes even to make music: 'I'm quite happy 'ere you know and coming to the pub is one of the ways to keep it like that. I've learnt to take the bad with the good and I know that, if I was somewhere else, I might be far worse off. Life's what you make of it wherever you are. You're never going to get anywhere by having everything you want delivered to your doorstep. I think we've got everything we need in these quiet, country villages to enjoy our lives. With good walks, fresh air, the pub and my music, it suits me down to the ground. I learnt the piano for a couple of years when I was very young. Then the war broke out and to carry the piano about as well as the rest of my kit was a bit difficult. So I chose to get a piano accordion. And that's how I started and I've been going strong ever since. I play at Clubs and pubs, for birthday parties and Golden Weddings. You name it and I've done it. One of my friends from the village of Fovant is called Bill Foyle and he's a good, old character – a bit like me. He sometimes comes and sings rural songs while I play. One of his favourites is called 'Down in the fields where the buttercups all grow' and I shouldn't be surprised if it was about the good old Nadder Valley.

Outside in the sun-baked street the sounds of the accordion and the strong Wiltshire voice attract customers to the Crown. Inside, it is cool and dark and the beer is flowing well. Regulars gather round and laugh as Arthur and Bill go through their well-worn routine.

IT is possible that on a quiet day Auriol Biddle could hear the music from her home at 3 Becket Street. It is part of a pretty terrace which overlooks Tisbury Church. Here, at the bottom of her garden, she cleans old milk churns and paints rural scenes on them. They are much in demand from collectors up and down the Nadder Valley. One of them stands proudly and colourfully on the bar of the Crown Inn: 'A few years ago somebody asked me out of the blue to paint a churn for them. I done it and I enjoyed it. It was put into a public house a bit away from here. Then I was lucky. Within four days somebody who'd seen it in the pub phoned up and said, 'Would you do one of those churns for me?'. So I thought how lovely and what a bonus. When I got to this gentleman's house I found that it wasn't one he wanted done but four. Then a few weeks went by and there was another four. And this lovely gentleman has kept me going for a long time. He was a dairyman once so, of course, he had masses of churns and other old-fashioned milking equipment, which will keep me busy for a while yet. The ones I've done are scattered all over Dorset and Wiltshire and off into Hampshire too I should

Not all country crafts are ancient in origin. Auriol Biddle paints rural scenes on old milk churns which are much sought after in the Nadder Valley.

think. People round here have begun to find out that I paint and so there's beginning to be quite a lot of interest. I first started painting when I was at school. Those years, unless you were very clever, you were kicked out at fifteen. And that's what happened to me. So I did all kinds of jobs but I kept on with the painting doing things for family and friends over the years'.

The sun slants down onto the terrace out of a Mediterranean sky. The flowers in the small garden are at their best and most colourful. Children's voices float up from the village, where they are splashing in the Nadder as it flows past the Church. Auriol sits comfortably by the edge of the hill looking out across Tisbury and the Valley beyond. On a turn-table before her stands a handsome milk-churn, which must date back to pre-war days. She applies heavy oil paint to the silver metal with strong hands and hefty brushes. She is busily building a stone wall and filling in the shadows between the beige stones: 'The churn I'm working on at the moment is a present for a friend, who lost her dog six weeks ago. The husband phoned to say that he'd got a churn and asked if I could paint the dog on it. The dog's on the front and I've put the husband on the back. I'm not sure how like the husband the picture is but, as he's been a shepherd most of his life, I've given him a smock and a crook. Years ago too she had a pet donkey, so I've put the donkey on the lid. It's a complete surprise for her. She doesn't know anything about it. Most of the paintings have a story of some kind behind them. It's not very often I do something out of my head. Usually when people come with their orders they have a pretty clear idea of what they are hoping for. Any that I do from my own imagination I usually keep for myself. The dairy-maids for instance are all my own. There's no doubt that they're idealised with their big shiny eyes and their rosy cheeks. A bit perhaps like you expect them to be in nursery rhymes or childrens' books. They're pretty and they've got no blemishes when in fact they certainly will have had calloused hands and weathered faces. But I won't have them like that on my churns'.

Everything in Auriol's house is neat and tidy, but there is no escaping her passion for old-fashioned milking parlours and the things which you find in them. Graduated jars, ladles, jugs and every shape and size of churn abound: 'It's difficult to get hold of them nowadays and, of course, people have begun to realise that they might be worth something. So they're hanging onto them more and more. And no one can blame them for that. So these things are getting rare and it's more usual for people to bring me things that they own and to ask me to do them. Always it's things to do with the countryside and perhaps that's because it's so lovely round here. I was born in the village and I've only moved from the top of the high street to the bottom during my life. In fact, I live now next door to the house that my mother, who comes from Reading, used to holiday in as a girl. So I love this country and Tisbury as well. There was a time in my teens when I rebelled and used to complain that nothing goes on here. But I'd never move now. I'm happy here with my friends and painting in the bottom of my garden'.

As the Church clock tolls midday, the deft fingers continue to apply heavy layers of paint to the churn. Overhead a flock of doves circles in the sunshine, clapping their white wings in the soft, summer air.

THE village of Chilmark is famous for its fine, honey-coloured stone, and many of the local houses are built from it. In the huge caves created from its quarrying, the RAF stores tons of bombs and munitions. John Needham's home is close to Chilmark and he makes his living as a potter and a stone-mason, spending much of his time working with the ancient rock: 'The vast majority of my work is very local indeed – within about five miles of Chilmark, all round the nearby villages. Sometimes there's other people working round about, but on the whole it's a fairly solitary occupation and it can be lonely. Often I see nobody all day. But I'm a bit of a loner anyway, so I enjoy working like that. And it goes for the pottery too. I first started that when I lived in Essex years ago. There was a wheel at home that my mother had and I sat down and tried to make a few things on it. Not much happened for some years but, since I've been living in these parts, I've developed it and at one stage it was my main rather poor source of a living. Now I do stonework as my main job and only make pottery occasionally. The stonework started when I built some walls for my mother's garden at Ridge. That must be about eleven years ago now. And I was asked by a neighbour who saw what I'd done if I could build a wall for her. She'd built walls in her time and knew a lot about the technique. She encouraged me to start up in this line of business. So I did some jobs in that area. And it slowly spread out from there. I hadn't intended to do it at all but it sort of took me over'.

The movements are slow and steady. The face is serious, the eyes enquiring, the hands tanned and roughened by the permanent, outdoor work. John is as economical with his words as he is with his strength. The rocks form perfect patterns as he puts them in place in the staggering August heat: 'There's great excitement for me in working on a wall that's probably been in place for hundreds of years and making your contribution to it. Those old boys knew what they were doing and they possessed great patience and skill. Often with an ancient wall a section falls down in a storm or because of tree roots or some earth movement and it's quite a challenge to repair them to look as they were originally built. And they were made very well indeed. There's a lot of dry stone walling round here although most of them were built using lime and water. But, whichever way, most of them are still standing and they haven't needed much maintenance over the years. One of my latest jobs was at a thatched Tudor house in the Nadder valley which had a sunken garden that had fallen into complete disrepair. The stone walls had all collapsed and had to be rebuilt, including one along the edge of the garden about a hundred feet long. New paths were added around the outer edge of the garden. It was all tumbled down and needed completely taking apart and rebuilding. And there's still some more to do there'.

It may not be finished yet but the garden is a dramatic sight with the summer flowers in full bloom and the stonework neat and tidy and symmetrical. Butterflies float across the paths and settle in the sun patches on the golden stone. John looks up from a pile of rock and allows himself the luxury of a moment's satisfaction as he looks at the weeks of work well done behind him: 'Shifting stone is heavy work – there's no denying that. But there are ways of doing it with crowbars and levers – tricks you learn through experience – and other ways of lifting it so that you don't damage your back. That lesson I learnt by doing in my back once and having to take a couple of months off. You might think that this would mean that it's a young man's job and you could be right about that I suppose. But I've just done one or two jobs that have involved very large stones and, if you use machines when necessary or get someone to help with the shifting, you can manage alright. So I don't think you necessarily have to be young – though like with most things it might help. What you do have to be is fit. That's certainly true. But I'm making it sound like a hard grind. There are great compensations and one of them is the real pleasure of working in this countryside. It's a most beautiful area with the rolling

59

John Needham from Chilmark makes his living as a potter and stonemason. His work is in much demand locally.

hills and the green valleys. And I love the stone buildings, which inspired me so much when I started out. I love the stone itself. I can quite understand why Chilmark stone has been so famous and has been transported far and wide. There used to be quarries all over the place including two or three at Tisbury and the one at Chicksgrove, which is now working again for building stone. It was reopened a couple of years ago which is an encouraging sign. So perhaps in the future the buildings round about will return to being made from local stone as they were in the past. The brick ones have only really come in during this century. I certainly think I have a feel for this stone and a confidence in handling it and I believe that's the reason that I've had some success'.

In a spacious farmyard John is slowly levering out the great rocks which make up the floor and which have sunk and shifted over the years. As he clears an area, he relays the stone to make it as it must have been when it was first laid. A white horse gazes solemnly out at him from a stable and bantams quarrel noisily at the entrance: 'This yard was built in the 1860s. I think it was well ahead of its time then, but a lot of the cobbles have come into disrepair and need attending to. The surrounding barns are being converted – the one where the hay was kept was burnt down and I've helped do some of the stonework on the buildings where it was needed or damaged by the fire. It's going to be a long haul this job. I come and go between other work. I've been at it here for a couple of years now and there's a year or two left yet. I can lay a few square yards of cobbles in a day and there's plenty of space to cover still. So I'm not going to be short of work for a while'.

The evening sun throws long shadows across the yard as John bends back to his labour. The stones he has set look like ranks of disciplined soldiers standing at attention and facing a rabble of untidiness where he has yet to lay his hand.

DIANA Forbes lives in seclusion on the high ground above Chilmark, where she teaches local children to ride. They come up early in the summer for their lessons before the flies and the heat can make the horses fretful and hard to handle: 'When I retired from teaching I'd managed to save up some money and I bought myself a retired hunter called Battle. I rode with a friend all round our bridlepaths, through Great Ridge Wood, Groveley Wood and Stockton Wood, round Chilmark and the nearby villages. I'd done it years before with my father who was very fond of riding. My pony at that time was Jerry, who sadly had to be sold when the war came. So I was keen on riding from that time and very interested in this part of Wiltshire. In those years I ran a small school in the house that I shared with my mother and father. But then my father died and my mother was old and I couldn't really run the school properly when she wasn't too well, so I decided to give the children twelve months to find other schools and started my riding school. There was good old Battle of course. And then there was a pony called Surprise, whose owners wanted her to graze in my meadows. When they left here they sold her to me and Surprise and Battle became great friends and that was how it began. Soon,

61

so many children wanted to come riding that I decided I'd have to get some more ponies. I steadily built up to five and a local farmer, who used to graze his heifers in the field, came up to make hay for me to keep the ponies through the winter. Now I've built it up to about twenty children coming here three or four times a week, mornings or evenings. More in the school holidays of course. They're very keen and I have a waiting list it's so popular. I always try to take Chilmark children but I have some from Tisbury too and Dinton and Fonthill Bishop. From time to time we have a gymkhana in the fields in the fine weather. They love that. And at one time there was another riding school started up in Tisbury but my children still came to me because I don't charge too much since they have to help out a lot'.

Indeed, in the early sunshine, there is non-stop activity round the trim, creosoted stables. Lavish grooming of much-loved friends, anointing with ointment where flies have bitten, cleaning of harness, saddling up, scurrying to and fro with buckets, brushes and brooms. Over all the chatter of young voices and the commanding sound of Miss Forbes encouraging, cajoling, reprimanding and teaching: 'Before they can ride they have to catch the ponies, clean them up and groom them, learn to saddle and bridle them and to be sure they're fit and well – and clear out the stables too. The children adore the ponies and are quite willing to make sacrifices for them. They have to learn early on to be gentle with them and to handle them patiently and with kindness. When a child first comes they're told that some ponies kick and some ponies bite so that they must always be cautious how they approach a strange one. They're told to talk to the ponies too because they like the sound of the human voice. And they must never show they're scared, which they needn't be if they do the right things. They must learn too to pick up their feet and to clean them, and this is another way they get used to the pony so that they're not frightened. Once they get on to the horse, the older children lead the younger ones round the field and I show them how to sit, to keep their toes up and how to hold the reins properly and to be gentle with their pony's mouth. And to get a really strong, secure seat so that they don't need to hold on by the reins, which is the last thing you must do. You can, if you must, hold on by the saddle if you feel insecure. Then, when they're big and tall enough, they must start to put on the saddles and bridles. This way, of course, the children get very fond of their ponies, so some of them become half-owners. But they're not allowed to sell them. When the time comes, I've got to have them back. One of the ponies goes over to Tisbury when I'm away and stays with its half-owner, which is a great help to me. The joy in it all is being able to explore the countryside in this way, to go through the woods and along the paths of our lovely, downland county and to introduce young people to this pleasure. And we try to help the farmers and landowners by always remembering to shut the gates. And, if we see any trouble like a sheep on its back, we'll turn it over. If we find any cattle escaped on the road we'll get in touch with the farmer and warn him. So we try to keep on good terms with the local people, who are good enough to let us go over their land'.

The sun is high in the sky now and horses and riders head back to the stables to shelter from the heat of the day. A buzzard circles slowly overhead keeping an eye on its territory. Across the valley sheep are being rounded up on their way to be dipped. Their calls bounce softly off the hills.

OVER the centuries men and women have admired the splendour that is Wiltshire. In 1798 the Reverend William Gilpin wrote of this special part of England: 'The ground is spread like the ocean. But it is like the ocean after a storm. It is continually heaving in large swells. Through all this vast district, scarce a cottage or even a bush appears. If you approach within two or three miles of the edge of the plain you see, like the mariner within soundings, land at a distance, houses, trees and villages; but all around is waste. Regions like this, which have come down to us rude and untouched from the beginning of time, fill the mind with grand conceptions, far beyond the efforts of art and cultivation'.

THE TARRANTS

THE eight Tarrant villages slumber along a decent Dorset valley close to the south-east of Blandford Forum. The little river Tarrant – rather charmingly taking its name from Terente, the trespasser – has regularly over the centuries flooded the meadows and the small hamlets on its eight mile journey from Tarrant Gunville, where it begins its travels, to Tarrant Crawford, where it empties into the grown-up river Stour. The summer of 1990 was so dry that the Tarrant was waterless, but the winter rains soon restored it to its normal, mischievous self. Squat-towered churches stand guard over the villages, and the farms and pastures lie peacefully in the autumn silence – the rush and tumble of harvest just a distant memory now. Above, the Dorset hills calmly await the storms of the bad months which lie ahead, and provide a comforting wall of protection to the people of the valley as they have done for a thousand years.

SINCE his fourteenth birthday Cliff Levens has worked at Home Farm, Tarrant Gunville. Now, sixty years on, he still travels there most days to harness his two good Shire friends, Prince and Royal, and to take them out ploughing or harrowing the fertile, Dorset soil. Their combined skills have won them many prizes in local shows and competitions: 'Prince was a rascal when he first come here. If you saw him then you wouldn't recognise him now. He was so naughty I couldn't even keep him tied up. It didn't matter how I did it, he'd get loose. He'd untie the rope, break it or do something. Then I started putting a chain behind him. That worked for a bit, but he soon found he could get back underneath and break out again. But I cured him in the end. I plaited some string in the top of his tail, put the chain in under and tied the tail onto the chain. Then he couldn't get back underneath. And that's what taught him to stay put in his stall. He's twelve now and Royal is fifteen. We had a bit of a problem with him too when he came 'ome here. He'd been messed up a bit by someone round his 'ead. It took him quite a time to stop him being nervous when you were working up front of 'im. Somebody must've been impatient in the past and slapped him about a bit if he wouldn't let them put the bridle on. Well, it took a while to get him out of being frightened about that. Even now, I'm the only one that can handle either of them about the heads, else they become jumpy. But you know, you wouldn't forget if it was you that had been roughed up – however many years ago it might be. Even though I was quite well treated, though not so well paid, I can remember clearly how I started working with horses when I was just a teenager. But I never done any ploughing until 1939. That's when I began, but only a little and that with a single plough. Later we had all double ploughs. In between I just milked the cows and did the other farm jobs.

Of course, the Guv'nor was an 'orse dealer in them days. Sometimes I used to have three or four different 'orses in a day to work. The old man would tell me to take 'em on up and to see how they'd go. If one went all right and didn't want no more training he'd take 'un and sell him on to someone straight away. And that's how it went on in them days.'

The stables are full of atmosphere and sparrows. Such places were a common enough sight on farms pre-War. The big wooden hay-racks above the feeding troughs, where the oats were poured, hung on the far wall above the high point of the sloping stone floor. The horses stood in passive rows, one hind hoof resting and one taking the weight. The rafters above were clothed in spider's webs and in ragged tufts of straw, which birds, rats and mice had pulled out of the thatch. The sound of the chomping jaws and the shifting hooves bring back instant and clear memories of those good times. The smells too are evocative – harness, dung, sweat and hay. They are honest sensations a million miles removed from today's chemicals and diesel, fertilizers and animal medicines. Such farming as that has served the land well for hundreds of years – men like Cliff Levens likewise: 'I got used to the tractors coming in the end I suppose and I done a lot of work with them too over the years. But I always enjoyed working the horses most of all and later doing a bit with 'em for exhibition jobs and ploughing matches. Won a few too. I go best if I'm in the class with the short turn ploughs. But if I'm up against the longer ones I don't stand as much chance. Because them long old boards puts it in place where the short ones push it in place. And that makes all the difference. Mine's 38 inches long. Sometimes I'm ploughing against a man with one 54 inches long, which is a lot of difference. Even so, I've beat 'em occasionally. The main thing about ploughing with 'orses may sound stupid but it's don't try and push the plough. Lots of people try to use it like a lawn mower without an engine. They seem to forget that the 'orses are up front there to do that. I once 'eard a man who reckoned he knew how to do it, telling some people that the way to keep the plough on the ground was to press on the 'andles. Well, he was absolutely wrong. You press down on the 'andles to get the plough out of the ground. But you know, if you've got a plough set up right and there's no stones, you shouldn't need to catch hold of the 'andles at all until you come to turn round. As far as the 'orses is concerned, the main thing is to break 'em right. Don't ever rough 'em. That's the way I look on it. Talk to 'em, which you've always got to do. People forget that nowadays, because you can't talk to a tractor. In fact, when I was eight or ten years old, there was an old fellow called Sammy Moore and he used to sing hymns all the time he was ploughing. Last time I 'eard of him he was down Christchurch way, but he must be a long time gone now I should think. You could hear him singing top of his voice miles away across the fields. And its not stupid, you know. It comforts the 'orses if they know for sure that you're still there.'

Up on the stubble the two great beasts heave against the harness as the plough bites into the autumn earth. It is October and the sky is grey and moist. The woods

65

and hedges are just beginning to turn. Nervous pheasants run for cover and the only noises are the clink of flints on metal, the straining of the leather and the old man's soft and encouraging voice: 'I like 'orses right enough or I wouldn't be doing this work. It's my 'obby as well as my job. It'll be sixty years on December 10th that I started. That's how clear I can remember. And I wouldn't have wanted it otherwise. Got used to it by now coming up here – and to this good countryside. The village has changed of course. Used to know everyone there one time. Now if you know 'alf a dozen you're lucky. But the land hasn't. And nor have the 'orses much. We had a horse here once. They called him Butler. And he'd run away with nearly everyone. There's a chap that lives down at Tarrant Hinton now called Peter Dyer – he'd always take off with him. Anyhow, the Guv'nor was down the village with him one day – and another chap too – and old Butler broke away with 'em. They galloped straight up past the farm 'ere. One of them was sitting up the front 'anging on. And he went up the headland – a good mile and a half from where he'd started and only stopped when he come to the ploughed field. Didn't like the look of the going there I shouldn't wonder. Funny thing was, he'd run away with any of them. But I could always manage him alright. He never tried it with me. It's strange but they know. And they have other ways too. The first pair of 'orses I had to drive on a single plough – before I was twenty that was – was on my brother's farm. And one of 'em suffered from cold shoulder or was what we call 'collar proud'. If I went in the field with him I couldn't put the plough into the ground and go straight on ploughing. First I had to drive 'em across the ground once with the plough out of the ground. Then he'd go alright after that. Otherwise he wouldn't pull. He'd just jack it in. Anyway, when I began, the old carter he started the headland round the outside of the field and I just followed and watched. Then he let me finish off the headland while he watched. And I finished them furrows and that was the first field I ever ploughed. I don't want even to guess at how many I've done since then. Some people say it must be lonely work. But it's not, you know. You're never lonely with them, are you? The horses I mean. And I live on my own anyway, so I'm quite used to it. And you're never by yourself in the countryside either. There's always something moving – trees, clouds, birds or animals. I think I'm lucky because it's beautiful even in the bad weather. I miss the elms and hope the other trees don't go the same way. But I don't want to be anywhere but Dorset.'

As dusk begins to shadow the hills the old man and the horses turn for home and shelter. They leave behind them the raw smell of newly-turned earth and the last of the rooks and gulls fighting over the feast which they have uncovered for them.

TOWARDS the bottom of the Tarrant Valley at Keynston Mill the Partridge family runs a successful fruit farm where people come from far and wide to pick their own. October is the grape-gathering season and the precious bunches are

The Partridge family run a successful fruit farm at Keynston Mill. Here Anni displays a fine crop of asparagus.

shipped to Somerset for wine-making. But apples, blackberries, raspberries, straw-berries and other good things are also still going strong and the farm shop is doing brisk business. Daughter Anni Partridge is an enthusiastic member of the family team: 'My father started the whole thing off growing strawberries only. It was very small in those days. Just half an acre. Now it's fifty acres of various kinds of soft fruit. And that's a lot to look after. The grapes came quite a bit later. That was another form of diversification along the way. You need to have a great variety of things to get people to come out here to pick and to buy. We'd been helping some people to plant vines in their vineyards on the far side of the river Stour from us. My father decided that it might be a good idea for us to have a go – another string to our bow, based on fruit but producing a completely different product in wine. Obviously you still need to have the right soil and to be the correct number of feet above sea level. So you can't just plant a vineyard anywhere you like in Dorset or any other part of the world come to that. But down the end of this farm there's a south facing slope and it has the right soil too. And the grapes are doing well. The tonnage that we got from last year's harvest was well above the national average though admittedly we did have a wonderful, long, dry summer, which the grapes like.'

It is a scene which is being repeated at the same time in France, Spain, Italy and Germany. Gangs of men and women in shabby clothes and eccentric hats move slowly along the vines picking methodically and carefully. Dogs lie bored on piles of discarded overcoats. A tractor, driven by a man wearing a high Spanish beret, mutters its way between the rows picking up the full containers. There is little talk and much concentration until the coffee-break when voices are raised in relief, stiff backs are stretched and laughter sets dogs' tails wagging. It is a surprise to find such a tableau in deepest Dorset even though the Romans brought their native Italian grapes to England two thousand years ago to make wine to help the legions get over their home-sickness: 'This year looked like being every bit as good as last year – until about three days ago that is. Then the rain came and fell steadily for more than forty-eight hours. It was very warm as well. During that time we got a tiny bit of mould in one of the grape varieties and it's been spreading like wildfire ever since. Luckily it's contained within one sort of grape and hasn't damaged the others. We've got six different kinds and our aim is to produce three different types of dry, white wine. In addition to that this year we'll have champagne on sale for the first time made from a blend of pinot noir and chardonnay grapes. It's very exciting, but a bit slow because it has to wait in the bottle for a year before it can be sold. It's a risky business though because weather like we've just had can knock a great hole in the harvest. We lost a quarter of those particular grapes in just a couple of days of warm rain. They are very delicate. They need to be nurtured all along the way. It's also a labour-intensive form of farming. But there we're lucky because people seem to enjoy coming to do the grape harvest. It's a bit of a party and there's a lot of fun too. Everybody has lunch together and gossips away. So that side of it is easy. But when it comes to the really hard graft of pruning or weeding it's not always quite so popular – and understandably so.'

The main house is centuries old and stands beside a great mill-pool close to the river Stour. A swan and her cygnets paddle and feed in the slow swirling water. A noisy mill-race tumbles into the pool, which is surrounded by a jungle of vegetation. Close by are the barns and the farm shop, which displays an elegance and a style which you would not be surprised to find in Bond Street. The warmth of your welcome however would astonish you compared to that of London's West End. Here are loaves of freshly made bread in all shapes and sizes, country baskets overflowing with dried flowers, local pottery, fruit and cakes and, of course, Partridge wine galore: 'Once we'd started producing a decent number of bottles of wine we decided that we needed somewhere here at Keynston Mill to sell it – as well as in other shops and outlets. So we came up with the natural idea of opening the shop. We already were taking cash and weighing things with the people coming to pick their fruit. So it wasn't such a big jump. Then I developed the idea from having the wine to sell to having things that go with the wine and try to compliment it. I hope it can go further still because it's a specially beautiful place this. Before we run out of barns completely we'd like to open a teashop – though we're waiting for planning permission on that. We'd sell wine by the glass there as well as normal teas. We're lucky because we draw people from that big area round Bournemouth, Poole and Christchurch. A lot come from Somerset too. Most come in the summer months to pick fruit. During the winter we rely on local trade. But it's a lovely spot to come out to in the fine weather. You can have picnics with the kids down by the river, gather enough fruit to stuff your deep freezer full and then off home again. It's a family day out and people enjoy it. They get personal service here as opposed to supermarket shopping and the satisfaction of feeling that they've done it themselves. Though I suppose there's a certain pleasure in feeling that you've escaped with your life from some supermarkets. Anyway, the demand is there I can assure you. Just come along in the summer and see. It's probably got something to do with Dorset as well. There's no denying that it's a very special county. When I was very young I didn't quite see it that way. I went up to London, finished off my education and worked in the theatre. I think I always knew I'd come back but I just had to pick the right moment. That came with the shop because I felt it was something I could do well and become involved with people I'd enjoy working with. I have to be honest and say that I don't think I'd much like pruning the raspberry canes or the vines all the way through the winter months. But here I am and I can't believe how lucky I am. This is a sane and heavenly part of the world.'

As customers pile out of their cars and throng the shop to buy early Christmas presents and fresh bread, Anni Partridge disappears into one of the barns to label some urgently needed bottles of wine. Outside in the yard bantams peck and squabble in the long grass beside the orchards.

ELLIOT Bailey has learnt over the years to turn his hand to most jobs with which the farms and estates in the Tarrant valley can confront a man. His home is at Tarrant Gunville and, in October, he is hard at work in the fields and woods of the local landowner. This has been his way of life since he left school nearly sixty years ago: 'I started in the 1930s and I've been lucky enough to earn my living in this village ever since. All those years ago I worked in the garden for the Squire, which was the grandfather of the boss I got now. I was only interrupted once. That was for five years in the army during the war. But I come straight back and carried on where I left off. I wouldn't have had it otherwise either. I know the place well and got plenty of interesting jobs, and know most of the people hereabouts as well. So I don't see I could have it much better. One of the unusual things up at the big house that I have to look after is the trees growing out the top of the stone arch up there. The arch must be thirty to forty feet tall and the trees, which are pines, are fifteen foot tall and more. They've been growing up out of there ever since I can remember and a long time before that too. Because I recall people who was very old when I was a boy telling me then that they had been there as far back as they could remember too. I suppose you get used to seeing them up there but people who come across them for the first time just can't believe it. They don't need much looking after but what they do want from time to time is a drop of water. It's not even every summer that they need it – only when it's been a very dry one and a long one like the last two years. Then we have to climb up long ladders, get the hose up there and give 'em a good splash. And they seem to appreciate it too. I don't think they grow quite as fast or quite as big as they would if they were in the ground. Then they wouldn't get the same amount of goodness, would they? But they seem to survive fairly well. Even though they're so exposed, they stayed up in all the gales and hurricanes we've had the last two winters when a lot of the great strong trees in the parkland come tumbling down. So they can't be that puny. When I'm up there hosing them I get the best views across this country. Being brought up in the countryside it's always been a big part of my life. I like the outdoors and from up on the arch I can see a lot of Dorset. And it looks good to me. People might say that they'd find what I do boring. But it ain't to me. How could it be with all of that to look at and to enjoy?'

From up on the top of a steep bank the farm yard where Elliot works looks as compact and comfortable as a child's toy. The buildings are tidy and symmetrical. Tractors and machinery, made small by the distance, stand in ordered rows. Near at hand, fat cattle and sheep graze the hillside. Rooks and pheasants add their voices to the farming sounds which float up from below. And in the distance is the clatter of a flock of geese. The old man walks slowly across to the nearby meadow with a bucket of grain in his hand: 'One of the many jobs I do is feeding the geese. We don't have that many of them. It's just that we 'ad a few to start off with. The reason we got them in the first place was that they were good at letting you know when strangers were about. If someone comes by they make a lot of noise like a watch-dog. Only difference is that you can't eat the dog at Christmas. Anyway,

'Summertime and the living is easy' for New Forest ponies in a pine plantation. It looks idyllic now, but, come the winter, the grass will have vanished and the wind will be knifing through the trees. Eat well now they must, for then it will be gorse and brambles only on the menu.

'A Robin Redbreast in a Cage
Puts all Heaven in a Rage'   *William Blake*

No such danger for this cheeky and independent chap, fluffing himself up against the fiercest winter frost.

they've gradually grown in numbers from four up to the several dozen we've got now. And that's making allowances for the few that get eaten each year. I can turn my hand too to most of the other farm work, except for the very specialised stuff. I don't do quite as many things now as I did when I was a youngster but I still keep my hand in. I've got some ploughing to do today. Used to work with 'orses one time, but we got this big, new machine now. We've not had it long. It's 215 horsepower and it can pull a big, old plough. If you get on good ground with it you can turn over about five acres an hour. So it's a bit faster now than it was with the 'orses. Ploughing for me is one of the most interesting jobs on the farm and one of the most important. If you get the ploughing right then the rest of your cultivations are quite easy to do. Way back, an old Dorset chap once said to me that the way you turned the earth over is ninety percent of the job. If you get it right, the rest is simple. If you get it wrong you've got trouble. And he was right. When you're out there you're always striving to make it that much better, to try and get it perfect, which is quite a hard job in some fields. Others are easy enough, but some just won't come right no matter how hard you try. But that's what makes it interesting. Trying to get the furrows straight too. We don't always succeed in that either, but we just struggle on trying to do the job better each time.'

High on the hills the old man and his tractor go methodically back and forth. The sun is close to setting. The autumn air is cold with the promise of winter. Timid fallow deer peep cautiously out of the surrounding woodland and trespass soft-footed onto the newly ploughed land disappointed to discover that young grass and new weeds, which were growing amongst the stubble have been denied them. The sky is light blue and tinged with the golds, yellows and pinks of the evening. Soon it will do down in a perfect, fiery orb: 'What matters to me is living somewhere where there's not so much hustle and bustle. In the mornings, when I come up here early, there's nobody about, nothing to bother you or interfere with you. You can do whatever you want without upsetting anyone. You have to go to work, of course, and do your job. But you're free and there's nothing to fret you – no noise or traffic or temper like there would be in the city. The countryside speaks for itself in Dorset. I'm sure there are many people who could make the case for where they live too. But this is special to me and I can't imagine anybody thinking it's not pretty good and that I'm not lucky. In fact, I think a lot of people would give their right arm to live in a place like we've got in the Tarrant Valley. I'm just pleased I can be here without having to give up one of my arms.'

KEN Cutler lives at Tarrant Rushton, where his garden and thatched cottage are a picture – even as late in the year as October. Up and down the Valley Ken is known as 'The Rat Man' because of his skill, learnt in his early years as a game-keeper, in controlling vermin and pests. Whether it's rats, wasps or the rapidly swelling population of rabbits, Ken is much in demand in the area: 'Old days people used to call me by my surname without any Mister even. Just Cutler this or

Cutler that. I never took very kindly to that. But now it's more Christian names, thank goodness. That's fair enough. Or Rat man, which doesn't worry me at all, because that's what I am. Social things like that have changed hereabouts and all for the better I should say. There's me and the dogs and the ferrets to do the work. They're the tools of my trade, I suppose. The dogs are both working terriers. The little black and white one I bred and sold. Then two years later it came back to me. But it had no idea about the work I was doing. Nor any training. But it took her about three months running alongside her old mother to learn all the work. And away she went from there. She started catching rats like a good'un with the old girl. It was marvellous really 'cos at one time I never thought she 'ad it in her at all, which is why I'd sold her on in the first place. The mother's always been brave though, even though she's lost a few teeth through age now and has more of a job to kill the rats. The other day I had this big, old rat going backwards and forwards round some bales at a farm. I couldn't see the dog but I knew she was waiting. In the end I walked up to the top and came back round the corner and there was the mother with this rat laying dead. He'd bitten her all right and she was covered in blood but the rat was worse off. Mostly we manage to keep on top of them with poison and even traps, but occasionally you get to places where only you and the dog can do it together. Another famous occasion I remember was when someone phoned me to say they had a rat indoors in their living room. So I went along with the two dogs. Everybody was sent outside and I closed the door. Well, we went round and round this room like cops and robbers. It took quite a while before we caught it. And you can imagine what a mess there was everywhere by the time we killed it. Terrible it was with the furniture and carpet. Better than having a rat in the house with you though. But that's quite an unusual thing to happen.'

While a tractor busily harrows the next door field Ken strides down a farm track in the October sunshine. There is mud underfoot and the two terriers daintily pick their way round the worst places. Over Ken's shoulder is a wooden box – the travelling home for two scrabbling and excited ferrets. In his hand is a well-worn spade and on the other shoulder a satchel full of nets, pegs and binder twine. At the end of the field is a mound of weed-covered earth where rabbits have made their home: 'The job's become instinctive to me really. I suppose I'm good at it. I should be by now anyway. I started as a gamekeeper boy for four years and the old man was pretty strict with me, so I had to learn a lot and fast. Next I had my National Service. Then I went with the Forestry for five years working in the woods. So I was learning all the time. From there I took on the pest job from the Ministry of Agriculture and did another five years for them. Then at last I thought I'd set out on my own and that was thirty-four years ago now, and I don't think I've ever regretted it. It might sound strange to some people but it's been an interesting life. Learning all the time. New traits. New poisons. New techniques. Travelling the countryside. Seeing so many birds and so much wildlife which most people wouldn't see rushing about as they do. I know this Valley pretty well by now – and the people in it. Some of 'em I get on well with. Others not so well. But that's how life is. And the satisfying thing is that there's quite a lot less vermin about here than there was when I started. That's not all down to me, of course. But I'll take my share of it. So can the dogs take theirs. And the ferrets too. I've kept them since I first started the job in the late fifties. Sometimes they've been not much more than pets when the rabbits had myxomatosis. There wasn't much call for them then, of course. But recent years there's been more use for them. And it's always been in my family. I was brought up with it as a boy. Father was dead keen on rabbiting. The ones we catch we try to sell, but there's a lot of them about now and folk have gone off them a bit since the disease years. Me too come to that. So we use them to feed the dogs and the ferrets too. Cheaper and better than that stuff you buy in tins.'

After flushing out and killing three or four rabbits, Ken sets out for home. The ferrets go back in their case to the satisfaction of the terriers, who watch triumphantly as their rivals lose their freedom. From the shed roof strings of giant onions hang down waiting to provide winter meals. Close by a skyscraper of a hornets nest stands on a shelf: 'I'm called out on all sorts of jobs – moles, mice, rats, rabbits, wasps and hornets. This is the time of year for the phone calls about wasps' nests. I certainly have no pity on them. They're devils. But hornets I don't make a habit of killing unless they're a real danger to people. They might be above someone's doorway or bedroom window and then, at night with the lights on, they come flying indoors and make a nuisance of themselves. They're quite rare at the moment and I'll only deal with them if I have to. But the wasps have been very bad indeed. To do the job, the main thing is getting peoples' trust. A lot of the work is done round peoples' homes and farms when they might not be there. So they've got to be able to rely on you to do what you say you're going to do and to come back as often as you need to. Over the years I hope I've built up that kind of trust and, if I have, that's half the battle and helps my work a lot. I suppose the saddest thing that's happened over my time is the way the numbers on the farms have fallen. When you go on a farm now it's very often there's noone there. You just wander around, do your job and out again without anyone to speak to. Years ago there was always crowds of people working. It's deserted now. But I, at least, carry on the same as I always have. Still suits me alright. I don't think I'd want to change to do anything else or to alter the way I work.

MAVIS Morse's home is at Number 11 Tarrant Rushton. But it is not just her home. It is the village shop as well. And it should probably be in the record books as the smallest village shop in the country. Tucked away by the back porch of her stone cottage, you would never guess as a passing stranger that it was there. Mavis, who was born in the Valley, has worked in the shop, which was started by her grandmother, since the '50s. Today, it's the only one left in the Tarrants: 'I'm quite busy all through the week. But things get busiest of all towards the weekend

Mavis Morse runs the one remaining village shop in the Tarrants from her home at Tarrant Rushton.

– Fridays and Saturdays. I hope I provide a useful service. Certainly plenty of people come by for a chat and a gossip. Those without phones have messages left here for them by their families. Village workmen drop in to get some lunch on their way to their jobs. And the old people without transport find it valuable too. So I'm a convenient place for them all to come. Especially for the old ones perhaps, because there's only one bus a week to Blandford and they often run out of something or forget to buy it. Anyway, I can sit in my back room by the stove if there's no customers. When the shop door opens I can pop out to serve. So it's very convenient for me too. In any case, I should be used to it by now – after more than thirty-five years.'

In her spare time and on Sundays, Mavis plays the organ at St Mary's church in Tarrant Rushton. It is a charming twelfth century building, hidden away down a track and shaped like a cross with all four arms the same length: 'I've been playing the organ here for over forty-eight years. My mother was the organist before me but she became ill. So I took over and have been playing ever since. It's a beautiful old church with a Norman tower and a window built for the lepers to look through from outside. In the summer quite a lot of visitors manage to find their way here to see it. The church and the organ are as special to me as the Tarrant Valley itself. They're all a part of my life and I couldn't really ask for anything more. I love making music for the people who live in this beautiful place. But I don't play every Sunday because the poor Vicar has all the churches in the Valley to look after. So there's one church of the five that doesn't have a service each week. Tarrant Rushton takes its turn with the others. But I miss playing those odd Sundays. There's so much lovely music.'

As the early Autumn leaves drift down from the surrounding trees, the organ can still be heard playing steadily away across the silence of the Dorset countryside.

The poet, Edward Thomas, who was killed at Amiens in 1917 during the First World War, walked this way over eighty years ago and might have been writing of the Tarrant villages and their valley in his poem, 'The Lofty Sky':

'Today I want the sky,
The tops of the high hills,
Above the last man's house,
His hedges and his cows,
Where, if I will, I look
Down even on sheep and rook
And of all things that move -
See buzzards only above -
Past all trees, all furze
And thorn, where naught deters
The desire of the eye
For sky, nothing but sky....'

THE OGBOURNES

THE three Ogbourne villages – St George, St Andrew and Maizey – nestle in the spacious downs to the north of Marlborough in the county of Wiltshire. The little river Og – named after a Saxon chief and often more of a dried up stream than anything that resembles a waterway – threads its course through the villages and joins the river Kennet close to Marlborough. That great explorer of the English downs, H. J. Massingham, came this way in the early 1930s and wrote: '... Here spreads the still but unquiet sea of giant trough and mighty fold and greater billow, the great, green sea of Wiltshire and Berkshire, to walk whose waves, restless in endless variation, yet brings tranquillity of spirit ... The villages, cushioned in by elm and beech and yet open to the spaces of sky and land, are a little oasis of the waste, umber-roofed from afar, white among their airy, many-cornered streets.'

ALICE Thorne and her sister Amy are in their seventies and have lived in the Ogbournes for most of their lives. They are among a group of people who keep village life going in the good old way. With Christmas just round the corner Alice is busy rehearsing her team of hand-bell ringers with carols for the festival. Another of the combined tasks is to clean and to care for the lovely old church in Ogbourne St George: 'I love the countryside because I was born and brought up on a farm. When we had to leave the farm we were lucky to find a house in Ogbourne and we had such a warm welcome when we came here that we've loved the village ever since. It's a special place this because everybody is so kind and helpful. We've never stopped since we came here. We're always doing something, working away or trying to raise money. We had to refurbish the village hall. That was thirty thousand pounds. Then the church floor went through. That was thousands. Next the church had to be rewired. That was another lot. But the villagers all pulled together and somehow we manage to achieve our aims. We came here in 1954 – thirty-six years ago now – and ever since then we've been involved in whatever is going on. They say country life is quiet but it's certainly not the case in these villages. It's non-stop activity here.

Inside the church the sisters raise a ladder against the west window. While Amy stands at the foot holding it steady, Alice climbs to the top with a long brush to sweep away dirt and cobwebs. It would be a risky job for a youngster but both ladies seem undeterred. After a while Amy reaches for her umbrella, which she has left on the font, puts it up and holds it above her head to stop spiders and dust falling into her hair. Alice reaches out to the furthest crevices to make sure that the job is properly done: 'The church is six hundred years old. Generations of people have worked hard over those years to keep it clean and well maintained. So it's up

Alice and Amy Thorne not only clean their village church, but also lead a team of enthusiastic hand bell ringers at Ogbourne St. George.

to us to do our part during our lifetime to try and preserve it for future generations. There's a good band of us who help with the cleaning and do the flowers and together I think we make quite a good job of it. As for climbing ladders, I don't mind that at all. When I was three years old my mother found me on top of the haystack and had to come and collect me. She was scared stiff. I've been climbing since I was born and it doesn't worry me a bit. I think Amy's more concerned about getting a spider in her hair. I quite enjoy the different view of the church from up here. I have been scared in my time though. Once when we were ringing the bells, the clapper fell out of the big one. It sounded like thunder on the ceiling above our heads and we thought that the whole lot was going to come down on top of us. I don't know who was last out of there but I promise you it wasn't me. Another time at Christmas we were ringing the bells for early service. We were all present and tugging away except the cowman. He was late because he was having to milk his cows before coming to church. We were managing quite well without him until he came dashing in at full tilt. One of the moving ropes caught him round the leg and hoisted him up in the air. As you can imagine, it really ruined our peel. Fortunately, with the hand-bells we use at Christmas, we don't have so many dramas. They were given to the village more than sixty years ago. There was a tale that they were found underneath a haystack. Anyway, nobody really knows where they came from or anything about them. They were old bells when they arrived and we're very proud of them. We've been ringing them off and on ever since. It's a lovely opportunity to get people together socially because hand-bells can be rung by all age groups. We've had children of twelve and younger all the way up to people of eighty. So it bridges the generation gap. One curious thing about them is that we've been told we mustn't polish them because it might spoil their tone. All we can do is to oil the leather straps to stop them perishing. Of course, the skills required to ring the hand-bells are totally different to what's needed in the tower. The big bells up there need strong men because the heaviest bell weighs nearly a ton. It's hard work to move that one. I can ring it if I have to when it's set up. But I can't ring it up in the first place. The hand-bells, of course, can be rung by anyone who is willing to learn. But there's one good thing about both. They bring people together from across the social divides. When I started ringing – over thirty years ago now – the captain of the tower was the roadman, whose job was to cut the grass verges with a hook and to mend holes in the road and to do other odd jobs. The other members of the team were a carpenter, the lord of the manor, the cowman and a retired naval commander. You couldn't get a much better mix than that, could you? When you're on the end of a rope, it doesn't much matter who you are. It's the bells that matter.'

As darkness falls, the two sisters finish their cleaning for the day, load the long ladder onto the top of their car and head back home to the other end of the village: 'They'll have to wheel me out of this place. I certainly won't go willingly. I can't foresee the future and a lot of what you can and can't do depends on your health.

We love it here and we're lucky to have a bus stop right outside our door so, if I have to give up driving, we can still get into Marlborough. But there's so much going on here that we don't need to go off into town for the pictures or other entertainment. We've got everything we could possibly want in the Ogbournes.'

EDITH Copplestone has lived in the Ogbournes for close to eighty years – and her family before her. She ran Edith's Café in nearby Marlborough for thirty-four years and is still a prodigious cook and a jam, marmalade and chutney maker. In the late autumn she gathers much of her fruit locally and sells her produce to the Polly Tea Rooms in Marlborough High Street: 'When I ran my café we did everything home-made. I think it was the fudge that eventually got me out of the red at the bank. Customers came in all shapes and sizes – famous and unknown, easy and difficult. One day a woman came in with her family and her little boy didn't like his cake. So she called the girl over and complained. They were always taught to fetch me if there was a difficulty. So I came along and asked her what the problem was.

She said: 'My little boy didn't like the cake.'
'Which one was it?', I asked. 'That one', she replied pointing to a dark brown one.
'Well', I answered, 'that's rum. It's written on it that it's rum. No children like rum cakes. Anyway, who's eaten it?'
'Oh, I did', she said.
'And you don't want to pay for it?'
'No, I don't'.
So I asked: 'Do you regularly go round to tea-shops trying to get free cakes in this way?'
She didn't like that very much as you can imagine. But she got her free cake all the same.

Edith moves back and forth in her kitchen cutting orange peel, slicing vegetables, labelling jars and stirring saucepans. On the Aga a huge cauldron of what will become strawberry jam seethes and simmers, filling the kitchen with sweet smelling steam: 'People have come from all over the world to try my jams. I've had Cary Grant in the shop, Lulu, Ray Ellington and many more. Lots of local people too, of course. An amusing thing happened once with my son, who was a pilot, and that got me lots of new customers. He wanted me to go up in his plane with him. But I wasn't very keen on the idea. Anyway, he persuaded me in the end. When I climbed in he asked me if I was nervous and I told him that I'd be all right provided that I looked out but not downwards. He then told me to talk to him to stop me thinking about being up in the air. Of course, it doesn't worry me to talk and he suggested that I should tell him about my jam and how to make it. So I went ahead and explained all the details to him. Well, we flew back to the aerodrome and landed safety. About a month later he had to go to a dinner for all

81

the people who were flying. At the end, the Chairman got up to make his speech and said that there had been an unusual bonus this year for all his ground staff. They all knew how to make strawberry jam now because they'd been tuned in to me while I was flying. I don't know if my sales went up after that, but I remember that I sold 2,800 pounds of jam the last year I was in my café. And that's over a ton, I believe. Even today I still make a big amount and nothing gives me more pleasure than to go along my shelves counting what I've got to see me through the winter. I have all my own recipes of course, which I've perfected over the years. For my marmalade I've always used three pounds of oranges and a quarter gallon of water, six pounds of sugar and two lemons. I like to cut the peel by hand because people don't like it too thin and they don't like it too thick. Then I cook the zest and the peel and the water together till it's reduced to half. You add the six pounds of sugar and bring it to the boil. I always time it carefully and give it twenty minutes. I think that's the secret. People tend to stick it on and just let it bubble. But you must have a real rolling boil – a good, old-fashioned gallop. None of your simmering for me. Next it has to stand for at least twenty minutes, otherwise all the bits come to the top. And then I bottle and label it – and that's it'.

THIS is famous race-horse country and the turf on the downs is as thick and springy and firm as anywhere in the world. The best thoroughbreds in the land have galloped and trained round the Ogbournes for generations. Gordon Richards, long before he became a Sir, used to live in a battered house above the villages and beside the gallops. For nearly a decade George Edwins was a jockey. Today, at his Foxlynch Junior Training Centre close to the Ogbournes and beside the main Marlborough to Swindon road, he teaches youngsters how to ride and to jump and leads them all the way through to international level. His pupils travel long distances to take advantage of his skill and his wisdom: 'I've ridden all my life. I did an apprenticeship in racing and did some of that and some show jumping too. I've been around with people who knew what they were about, and you begin to pick it up, of course. There are some people who have cracked most of the problems. Nowadays, when someone new comes to me to learn, it usually only takes a short while for me to tell if they're going to be any good. Sometimes I'm wrong of course, and they surprise me. But there's something about them that makes you look again, that draws you back to them. Then what you do is to watch them carefully all the time because you want to prove that what you thought in the first place was right. Then you take it from there with lots of training and plenty of hard work. Of course, there's problems all along the way. It wouldn't be any fun if there wasn't any. I suppose the biggest difficulty every child's got are the parents. They're all nice enough people but they tend to get in the way and to mess the job up. Like the children, they need to be straightened up a bit. They get too keen really, keener even than the children. They want the child to do well and then they get visions of lots of money. It's that that's spoiled it as much as anything and taken a bit of the pleasure away from the sport'.

The stable yard is immaculate. Wembley and Earls Court badges decorate the doors. Rosettes cover the ceilings in a colourful display. Much loved ponies of every size are being groomed and harnessed. Young girls with wise eyes examine every detail as they work. These are already determined professionals and sure that they are going to make the grade. George moves from rider to rider checking that everything is in good order and up to his high standards: 'The last two years have been particularly good. I've had some really talented youngsters come this way. And I'm fully booked up now for the next year. I don't teach people to ride. I teach them to be effective show jumpers. Your best jumpers aren't always your best riders. The thing in show jumping is that you must be effective. What it's about is winning classes. It's the technique of riding to fences and the right attitude to them. I try to teach them about getting their feelings and their wishes through to their ponies, so that the horse can then do the job. Once they've learnt that they can practise themselves. I think this is what they come here looking for. Then I try to get them into a work pattern constantly from day to day and from week to week, and to let the job come together as quietly and as smoothly as possible. When you come to the competition itself, there's certain days you go out and you know that, whatever you do on that particular day, you won't be wrong. So that's the day you win classes. Another day you go out and nothing comes together at all. No reason for it that you can see. It happens to everybody. The days you can't even drive to work properly. Those times you just sit and let it happen to you and hope that it will come right next time.'

In the meadow the riders take it in turns to practise over the jumps. George's daughter, Amanda, is in charge of the smaller girls, who show every bit as much discipline and determination as the older ones. George and Amanda shout commands and instructions and watch every move and nuance of the riding with eyes that give nothing away. They size up every approach, register every moment of fear, acknowledge each successful achievement: 'Their biggest aim and ambition at the moment is to qualify for Wembley – the leading Junior School Jumper in the Horse of the Year Show. It starts around Easter with the qualifying rounds up and down the country and gradually builds up from there. I specialise in qualifying them and I think I must have done more than anyone else – well over thirty by now. That's the hardest bit. Once they've done it they can enjoy the day and get out of Wembley whatever they can. But it's something for them to get there whatever else happens.'

High on the Marlborough Downs George leads his pupils up a steep track onto the Ridge Way – the oldest road in England. The wind chases the clouds across the November sky. Sheep and cattle spook and then relax again as the cavalry passes by. Even on a hack like this George is alert for any lessons that he can pass on: 'This is terrific horse country. There wouldn't be four places in England as good as this. We live at the bottom of the Downs. If it's possible to give a horse an hour's work in twenty minutes this is the place to do it with our steep climbs. We don't have to use the roads very much. If you get a horse which is a bit strung up or nervous a couple of months up here relaxes them and calms them down. There's plenty of variety too. I can ride six horses in a day and not go down the same track. We even ride at night sometimes and then the deer come out on the path and run along beside you. It's almost too good to be true.'

ARCHIE Barrett lives beside the river Kennet at Axford – a few miles to the south – east of the Ogbournes. His family has known and loved this countryside for generations. Archie is a jack of all trades – woodman, hunter, estate worker, beater and loader – but he specialises in jobs along the river, building the banks and keeping the sluices running, cutting weeds and feeding the trout. He is a country-man through and through: 'What my friend Bob and I have got to do this morning is to put a new sluice and hatchway into a stretch of the Kennet. Instead of doing it in oak like we would have done in the old days, we're doing it in iron. So it's damned heavy. We've measured it up and I hope it's going to fit perfect. Then we drop the hatch in and the depth boards and, Bob's your uncle, we can control and maintain the depth of the water. That means it will improve the river and the fishing and help us in our aim to create a small lake upstream. It'll all be brown trout here. We don't spoil a river like this with no rainbows. We didn't have no schooling for this type of work – none at all. We'd just been born into the estate ways I suppose. We picked it up here and there from old rivermen and other workers. It's not something you can get out of a book. That's why it's hard to explain. Each job's different, so there can't be hard and fast rules. It's been handed down from father to son for generations. Bob's father was my tutor and Bob and I have grown up together here. Now and again I seem to come up with some wild idea or other. Then Bob's got to scratch his head, do some welding, which he's very good at, cut the pieces and put them together and we hope somehow that it will all go right. One thing we don't need to bother about though is this part of the world. You can't beat it. There's an old Australian I know. He come across here. When he went home he was having a drink with some friends and telling them where he'd been. Well, one of the lads had been a pilot round these parts during the War and he said: 'Harry, how the hell did you manage to get there? That's God's own country.' And he was right. You can travel wherever you like in the world, but when you come back round this area, you don't ever want to leave again. I shall be pleased if I can die on this bit of water with a rod in my hand or just looking out at the river. That'll be a good way to go.'

While the two men work in the water creating ripples which flash and sparkle in the winter sunshine, a small brown and white Jack Russell terrier explores the banks and noses his way through the rushes. Now and again he stops, his head held high and alert, one front foot lifted delicately off the ground. Then a moorhen or a coot dashes for cover and the dog prowls on. Every few minutes he returns to where the men are working, surveys the scene briefly and then continues his hunt: 'Oscar's with me all the time. He's a good, old character too – a bit like me. We've had some adventures together. One day I was setting some mole traps. I was across the other side of the water and Oscar drove a rat out – not a vole, a nasty great rat. Well, he jumped into the water and swam after it. I ran across the bridge nearby and picked up a stick and tried to hit the rat. But the damn thing broke. So now it's up to Oscar. Well, he's only a little chap and only his ears and nose was above the water. As he comes up to the rat, he grabs at it, but all he done was to catch hold of his front leg. Course the rat straight away got Oscar by the nose and was hanging onto him and beginning to drown the dog. I didn't know what to do cause he'd gone under a couple of times. I thought I'd just have to go in even though it was deep there. But I had some money in my pocket and I'm a bit careful about things like that. So I chucked the notes down on the bank and was just about to jump in when Oscar with his last bit of energy heaved himself onto the bank. He was so exhausted he just stood there for a bit with the rat dangling on his nose. He couldn't do anything. Then he took a big gasp of breath and that was the end of Mr Rat. He scrunched him up blooming quick. Anyway, that old rat must have put some poison into him or something 'cause Oscar nearly died that night. But he pulled through and he's as good as new again now.'

In a secluded spot close beside the Kennet Archie goes to feed the trout and to make sure that everything is in order. The water churns and thrashes as the fish come to feed. In the distance a heron hunts sedately by the bank while a flock of geese glides in to land. A fine, old mill stands nearby and the water creams down the race beside it. Below, black and white swans rest and feed: 'I look after two lakes beside the river. They're wonderful places. I do all the banking and trimming, look after the fish, keep an eye out for trespassers and sometimes go fishing with the gentlemen. I'm hard put to it to describe how I enjoy this life. You're never going to make a fortune at it. That's for sure. But it's something someone with a fortune envies. The work itself may not sound much but it makes me contented. I got to keep the weed under control and get rid of vermin like pike or mink. Got to check the fish regularly to make sure there's no trouble with them. And, of course, if the water isn't controlled with all these sluices, which have to be maintained, all you'd have down through the valley would be a muddy ditch. So there's more to it than meets the eye. We're losing the water too fast now off down the Thames. If it rains today, no matter how hard, it's off down the river tomorrow and into the sea. It's got no time to sink in because the ground's all hard and patted down after the dry summers. I don't think our water table will come back until we've had a good, deep snow – something that will go slowly into the chalk as it melts and bring it back up to the old levels. I've learnt about these things over the years. I often think it was born into me, because I started my life right there beside the river and, as a boy in the village, I used to go round with the old keepers. They'd done the same with their fathers – back as far as anyone could remember. All village lads and all doing the job by instinct as much as anything. When I was a lad there was just three landlords on the river from here right through to Marlborough. If any of the keepers didn't get things right on the water, the three gentlemen would get together and whoever it was would be in trouble. Nowadays I suppose there could be twenty different owners up through the valley and it makes it all that much harder to look after and to control.'

As long as there are men like Archie Barrett on the Kennet the river will be in good heart, whatever the problems may be. Hand such a precious stretch of water to the scientists or the experts and they will deny it the care and the experience which it so badly needs. While the water fowl sit serenely on the lakes Archie and Oscar walk along the bank on their way to their next job and more adventures.

ELDIE Merrett and his son are the Ogbourne builders working, whenever they can, with the local stone. Men like them have been collecting flints from the farmers' fields for a thousand years — the result, better crops and beautiful buildings. One perennial job for the father and son is to maintain and mend the almost mile-long wall round the Manor House in Ogbourne St George: 'It's been here four or five hundred years I would think. It's all local stone that's come out of the ploughing over the years off the fields on the downs. To bind the stone together they'd grind up the chalk. That's all they had in those days. Mixed it with water, stirred it up and just lopped it in there. If it's kept dry it should last a hundred years and more, which isn't too bad by modern standards. The wall's made up of all kinds of stones — anything they could lay their hands on really. Then every now and again there is a key-stone — a great big one which is the width of the wall and which stops the thing coming apart and separating. It serves the same purpose as a 'tie' in a modern wall. The reason we have to mend this one so often is wear and tear. You've got to expect it after all those years. It might be a tree root shoving it out of place. You have to deal with that and then rebuild. Or, more often perhaps, the jointing between the coping stones on top gives way. That allows the wet to get in and, with a severe winter, the thawing out makes it expand and pushes it all over the place. Again, we have to pull it all down and start over again rebuilding and strengthening. It looks an awkward job and you need to know what you're about. But, with a bit of experience, it doesn't take as long as you might think. You mustn't tell the person you're working for that though.'

The two men create a minor landslide as they crowbar a sagging bulge out of the beige stone wall. They jump aside as big boulders roll down towards them. Pigeons fly in fright from the beech trees by the Manor House. Like dentists, Eldie and his son make sure that all the loose stuff is cleared before they start to rebuild painstakingly and with the relentless rhythm of country workers: 'It was about ten years ago when we were working on a boundary wall much closer to the big house. We found a skeleton in there with about eight foot of wall above him. Whether he didn't work hard enough and they buried him on the job or whether he died and they couldn't be bothered to take him to the churchyard, we just don't know. But it was an old skeleton and it had been there a long time. Seemed to have done a good job in the wall too. Never found much else but that. A few old coins now and

Eldie Merrett builds and repairs beautiful walls from local stone and flint in the old traditional manner.

then. But I think they were all poor in the days when they built the wall and they wouldn't willingly leave any money behind them.'

High on the downs above the villages the November wind probes the warmest clothes. The two men work steadily gathering flints and shaping them for their next job. The views across Wiltshire and into Berkshire are spectacular. The clouds chase one another eastwards. Across the field the sound of metal on stone must have been heard up here since the Iron Age when man first began to use these stones for building: 'We just pick 'em up as we need them. There's plenty up here for a few centuries yet. The plough keeps on turning up more. The skill in it is finding the shape of flint which you need and looking for a 'face' on it. It's the same with the sarsen stones which were used in the wall. The strength is OK but you need them to look good as well. So we have to do some napping while we're up here – chipping at the flint to give it a good front to face outwards. A lot of 'em have a natural face to them, but there's many that have to be worked on too. When you've been at it for a while you learn how to hit them just right so they split perfect. Like someone who knows how to do the job splitting wood. One of my best hobbies is walking up on these hills and that's how I find good collections of flints. Then the farmers leave them up on the sides of the fields for us and we're able to buy them off the farms in cart loads. That's how it's always gone on. I've been here since I was two. I was brought up in a little hamlet close to the Ogbournes. 1923 it was when we came. I've been walking the downs since I was ten and I still haven't got fed up with the place. I'm still seeing new things every year too. The main thing I've seen over all those years is how much of the downland has been ploughed up. The wildlife has changed a bit too, perhaps because of spraying and chemicals. You never see so many big coveys of partridges like we used to years ago. Fifteen and eighteen in a bunch them days. You don't see so many peewits or plovers either. Far fewer skylarks over the downs too, though they're still lovely to see and hear. Less primroses and cowslips along the side of the woods because they've all been dug up and cultivated. There used to be masses of them in my young days. But it's still good enough. A bit sharp this time of year mind you. 'Ealthy weather – very 'ealthy indeed. Lots of fresh air, which means you've got to walk a bit faster and work a bit harder to keep warm.'

HERE on the high ground in November the most stubborn mental cobwebs are easily blown away in the fresh, prevailing winds. Winter is nearly here and the sky is a chaos of racing clouds on collision courses. The hills themselves seem washed and smoothed by the wild weather. H J. Massingham wrote of the scene with the pen of an artist: 'The Wiltshire plateau covers so wide an area and most of the villages are so warmly boxed away along the river valleys that you have the illusion of seeing into distances without ever looking below you. It is as though you were striding over the clouds without getting a glimpse of the earth beneath, and yet the eye can follow the fleecy masses to the limit of its capacity.'

THE CHESIL BEACH

THE great Chesil Bank sweeps like a pebbled highway for more than ten miles along the Dorset coast from Portland, past Abbotsbury and on to Burton Bradstock. There is some argument about where the Chesil ends and the beach beyond it to the west begins. What seems sure is that, when the fog is down, fishermen landing on the shingle can tell almost exactly where they are from the size of the pebbles underfoot – the large ones at Portland and the small ones to the West. Chesil is the old word for these small stones and this must be one of the greatest stacks of them in the world. It is a unique creation of Nature and a symbol of the awesome power of the sea, which has piled it up over the centuries.

At the eastern end the great wall is nearly sixty feet high and two hundred yards wide at its base. Yet the waves have often smashed over this barrier and flooded and ruined the houses behind it. Even when the breakers do not come over the top, their force sometimes pushes great geysers of water through the stones, erupting into the relative calm on the far side. During a memorable storm in 1824 the water is described as pouring over the bank at Fleet as fast as a galloping horse and at a depth of thirty feet.

Behind the Chesil shelters some of the best of Dorset – the Bride Valley with its green downs, thatched villages and old-fashioned farming. It is the countryside of old England and still breeds some of the great characters, whom Thomas Hardy described with such clarity and pride. He came here in 1879 when the wreckage of the great storm over fifty years earlier had still not been cleared. He wrote in his diary: 'As to the ruined walls in the low part of the Chesil, a woman says the house was washed down in the November gale of 1824. The owner never rebuilt it, but emigrated with his family. She says that in her house one person was drowned (they were all in bed except the fishermen) and next door two people. It was about four in the morning that the wave came.'

MEN have been fishing off the Chesil Beach back into the mists of time. Crossing the fleet – the stretch of water between the Bank and the mainland – in flimsy punts, they have cast their nets into the English Channel and been well rewarded. Today Maurice Connelly from Langton Herring carries on the tradition and knows the Chesil and its moods as well as anyone along this dangerous coast. The fish are not as plentiful as once they were, but the challenge is the same as it always has been: 'This is a rough December day. No mercy in the wind or in the cold. So much of fishing depends on the weather. We can rarely get afloat this time of the year to shoot the nets. In between the storms, if you're lucky, you can sometimes get two or three nice-sized fish. Unfortunately though, you more often get days like today when you catch nothing. But that's fishing, isn't it? To be honest, it's unusually poor at the moment. In fact, I've never known it quite so bad. For some reason, it doesn't seem to have picked up since last winter's gales. There's probably no scientific reason for that. But it seems to be the case. Today's weather is bad enough, but it's often even worse with a lot more sea and heavier waves. The good time is in the spring when the mackerel come in. They always arrive at the Portland end of the Chesil and then slowly work their way west up the beach to Chickerell, Fleet, Langton Herring, Abbotsbury and then on up to Burton Bradstock. That's a good fishing time for us.'

The great breakers unwind onto the shingle with a crash of foam and spindrift. The sound of the pebbles rolling back with the water is like the rumble of a distant avalanche. Maurice and his friends are wrapped against the weather, but nothing made by man can keep them warm in these exposed conditions: 'We've had lots of adventures, of course. Some of them have had a funny side to them. I remember once, some years ago now, that we were over here on the Bank having a coast-guard drill. We had a batch of rescue rockets to fire and one of them was a bad 'un. It didn't ignite – not straight away. It took a second or two. Well, it went roaring along the shingle where it had touched down and hit a boat that was sitting there half-way up from the sea. The rocket went straight through the boat and came out the other side still with the line attached to it. We all laughed, but then the boat didn't belong to any of us, did it? The job's not always as exciting as that though. Usually it's just the normal routine. I started fishing when I was ten – it must be forty or so years ago now. I came over with the seine crew that was fishing for mackerel in those days. That was in the summer months. We used to come over the Chesil in the evenings after tea when the men had finished work. A lot of the fishermen in those days had day jobs at the local brickyard at Chickerell and they used to ride over here on their bikes. Then, after the night's fishing, they'd ride back. Or sometimes the fish lorry would give them and their bikes a lift home for most of the way and then they'd pedal back to their individual houses and on to work. So there wasn't much time for sleeping. But it didn't matter a lot because there was lots of fish, and that kept your spirits up even if you was tired. Trouble is now that the fish has been getting less every year. I don't really know why it is. Partly over-fishing, no doubt. But I think it's more far-reaching than that. I just don't think anybody really knows the answer. But there's still some fish to be had and still competition between the fishermen. Years ago there was quite a lot of rivalry between local crews. When the fish were in one particular part of the Beach the men would all travel there. Early in the season they'd do down the eastern end. Later on, around August and September, they'd be up at Abbotsbury and everyone would go there. Obviously, the crew that could get in first often had the best shot. So there was quite a lot of dashing about. And it was good fun and exciting too. I wouldn't do it otherwise. I have done it all these years and it's become a way of life for me. But I'd never fish if it wasn't enjoyable. You certainly wouldn't do it for the money you get out of it.'

Enjoyment is not the first thought that comes to mind as the men haul their long net hand over hand from the raging sea. Portland stands grey and daunting in the distance. Wind, waves and weather combine to create a noise which makes speech almost impossible. Maurice's face is largely hidden behind a leather cap with big ear-flaps tied tightly down under his chin. Only the eyes can be seen as they look keenly out towards the breakers, from which the net is slowly emerging: 'The biggest fish we ever had was a basking shark. It was February – a bitter cold day. We was hauling it in by hand because we had no winch in those days. I kept on saying, 'The nets coming hard today. Whatever have we got in 'ere?' All of a sudden this huge shark broke the surface of the sea. It made us jump a bit, I can tell you. We pulled it in, untangled it and, as it was still alive, we let it go. It was seventeen or eighteen feet long but quite docile and harmless. Another time I got a lovely bass – a big coloured one, what we call a 'sparkler'. I caught it several years ago in a trammel net and it weighed about seven pounds. I had it mounted and I've still got it at home now. I'm proud enough of that but much bigger have been taken along this stretch. After all, people have been fishing off of the Beach for generations – certainly back to the tenth or eleventh century. There are records going back that far to prove it. People don't really fish for a living here now, whereas a century ago and in the even earlier times they undoubtedly did. The thing that won't have altered much is the conditions. It's hard now as ever it was. I've known it so freezing that the pebbles are frozen together solid so that they're like concrete. Then it's dangerous for us because it's slippery and you've got a job to stay on your feet. The trouble is the weather's so hard to predict. You can't tell ahead what it's going to do. You can come over one evening and shoot the net off thinking it's going to be a quiet night. And the next morning it's impossible – a bit like today. That's why we always leave a rope ashore so that we can pull a net in if conditions get bad.'

Once the net is safely stowed away the men trudge back towards the Fleet on their journey homewards. Walking through shingle is hard work and the sort of exercise which professional boxers might relish. Maurice has been doing it all his life and makes easy work of it: 'In the winter months years ago we used to spear eels in the Fleet with a flat-headed shaft called a peck. Those days – over thirty years ago now – prices were silly and you used to get only a shilling or two for eels. But then you could catch ten or fifteen pounds weight in a day. And, of course, to the people that were fishing for a living, that was quite a bit of money. On the Fleet, punting is easier than rowing. It's a tradition that's been carried out behind the Chesil Bank for hundreds of years. All the boats had quants or poles and poked their way across. You can cope better on the mud-flats like that. The water's very shallow all the time here and especially on the low tides. The good thing about working on this bit of water is the views of Dorset beyond – the rolling hills and the unspoilt beauty. It's something you take for granted if you're not careful. But I think it's probably why I've only moved a mile in my life, and I certainly don't plan to move any further now.'

DURING the summer months Donald Peach takes visitors from Abbotsbury to the nearby Swannery in his pony and trap. In December there is less temptation to use this form of transport, but the views across the Chesil Beach are still magnificent and the surrounding scenery as enticing as ever. Donald has known it well for decades: 'I lived at the coastguard station overlooking the Chesil Bank for thirty years. We were about two hundred yards away from the Fleet – a little bit further from the Bank itself. It was a dangerous enough place in the days of sailing ships, but not so bad since with motors and steam. Those early days I did a lot of fishing for mackerel from April to September. So I was home when the cold winds blew. I left school at fourteen and got a job at the local forge. The war was on at that time. Fish were in great demand and we used to go netting them at four o'clock in the morning, get home at half-past seven, work with the blacksmith at eight, knock off again at half-past five and then back over on the Chesil Beach again until midnight. We used to pray for the wind to blow sometimes so we could get some rest. But, because of the need for food in wartime, we had to keep it up no matter how tired we was. Well, after the fighting was over, we just carried on. There wasn't the same urgency then though. It still goes on now and the fish are still there. But the interest and the need are less. So I suppose I've got the pony and trap now to replace the fishing in a way. I started with horses in 1942 and I've always had an interest in them. Then about ten years ago this opportunity came to work with them again down at the Swannery and I grabbed it. I'm allowed to keep my wagon in the great Tythe Barn at Abbotsbury and I thoroughly enjoy the job.'

In the December drizzle the strong cob pulls the cart through the doors of the barn and onto the cobbles. In front is a pond populated by coots, ducks and moorhens. Donald sets out at a slow trot along the narrow Dorset lane which takes him towards his childhood fishing grounds: 'When we were looking for a horse for this work we were put in touch with a lady on a farm in Tewkesbury. She did a lot of horse-dealing with Ireland. She'd been there recently and had come back with six driving horses. This was in February ten years ago now. Well, she rung up everybody she knew that wanted to buy horses and told us she'd be selling them on the Monday morning. On Saturday night in Dorset and right across the West of England we had heavy snow. When Monday morning came almost all the roads were still impassable. So we didn't get away to Tewkesbury till Tuesday and we didn't arrive there until after lunch. We found the farm house, knocked on the door and the lady come out and said, 'I'm sorry. I've already sold five of the horses. There's only one left.' Well, that was quite a disappointment. Anyway, I said to her, 'Could you bring 'im out and we'll have a look at 'im?' And out came this big, fifteen-two grey, which was just what we was looking for. So we never see the other five and don't know what we missed. But we found the perfect horse for the job first shot and felt very lucky. Trouble is, the horses are inclined to get a bit rusty during the winter lay-off. We've got two and one of 'em is ridden quite a lot. Driving horses in the winter with a carriage is cold work. So we generally forget about it by the end of October. Then they're quite pleased to get out of the field and back between the shafts once the spring comes round again – even if they may have forgotten some of the skills. Driving horses in the good weather is a wonderful pleasure. You've really got to do it to appreciate it. You're trotting along the road, you can hear his hooves and the cart's swinging a little bit, the sun's shining and the sea's just over the meadows. It's a grand job and I feel very fortunate. As long as I'm somewhere I can look over and see the water, that's all I want. We always try and drive along the coast so that we've got the sea on one side. And the visitors we carry enjoy that too. We meet people from all over the world – not just English. It's interesting because the majority of the Europeans who come to Abbotsbury speak good English, so we can talk about where they come from and how they're enjoying this country. But you can get caught out sometimes. I had an example a few years ago when a lady and her daughter came up to me while I was waiting to pick up some passengers. The girl was about twelve and, when she spoke to me, I didn't understand a word she said. So I turned to the mother and spoke to her quite slowly: 'I'm very sorry. I only speak English. Which country do you come from?' And she said, 'We come from Birmingham.' So that put me properly in my place.'

Donald still works as a blacksmith today in the same forge where he was apprenticed all those years ago. It stands beside the Elm Tree pub in Langton Herring and there he makes tiny carts for Shetland ponies to pull, old-fashioned shepherds' crooks and mends implements and iron-work for the villagers: 'The genuine farmwork for us blacksmiths has all gone now. But there's still business. The work I do, in spite of all the smoke and heat and steam, looks very simple. The thing is I've been at this sort of trade for a few years now and I've done most of the jobs thousands of times. So it's probably not as easy as I make it look. The shepherd's crooks, for instance. I learnt to do as a boy almost. We sold quite a lot of 'em in those days and this forge had a good reputation for producing them. They went all over Dorset from here. The work is all done by hand and eye. There's no ruler or exact measurement. You just cut the metal the length of the anvil when you've finished them and that's accurate enough to make the complete job. When I first started out, the vast majority of the business was for farms and at least fifty percent was shoeing horses, mainly heavy working horses. That's all gone now but I still carry on with the shepherds' crooks. Start to finish they take about two and a half hours each. So you don't get many done in a day. But it's good work and I enjoy it well enough. And, as for Dorset, I've had a wonderful life here and wouldn't go anywhere else.'

Dusk comes early in December. By four o'clock the warm glow from the forge is already shining in the gloom across the village street. From inside, the sound of metal on metal echoes off the walls of the old cottages. Through the windows of the houses Christmas lights gleam and sparkle, and wood fires flicker. The smoke from the chimneys is barely visible against the darkening sky.

HIGH above Burton Bradstock at the western end of the Chesil Beach the Knightsmith family lives in old-fashioned splendour at Norburton Hall. Their home has become a social mecca for the village and for the Bride valley. On a December morning the British legion meets for a friendly skittles match under the supervision of Felicity Knightsmith in what was once the old stables: 'My sister and I were always keen members of the WI team. We could never play enough. We wanted a practice alley and we couldn't get one down in the village because they wouldn't give planning permission for it and the local people said that it would be too noisy. So we said, 'Let's do something up here at the hall and build a private alley which we won't hire out.' We only play here with friends and with the WI team. The building the alley is in was a very old barn without a roof but just the right length and shape for skittles. Our scout leader, who was also a builder, helped us a lot and provided the wood we needed, which cost us a hundred pounds. Then we had the job of putting the roof on, and next the electricians came in. And that was more than a thousand pounds. But it's given us hours and hours of pleasure and we have regular friendlies for husbands and wives and anybody who likes to play. Other times the team practices, and it's a wonderful game because children can take part just as well as grown-ups. Unlike other sports, it's almost impossible to learn skittles. There's so much luck involved. At any rate I've always found it difficult. I was a keen tennis player and liked most sports. With all of them you can learn and improve. But with skittles it's just the mood you're in. If I'm honest, I'd have to say there's a lot of luck about it.'

The wooden balls roll down the plank floor and smash into the tall, chipped skittles at the far end. Nearly twenty villagers crowd the building. Coffee, tea, wine, cakes and sandwiches are in plentiful supply and the sound of conversation nearly drowns the noise of the game. Sometimes there is a roar as somebody knocks down all the big pegs or misses them altogether: 'We had a boy up here the other day to take the place of brother Nick and to be a sticker-up – the one who replaces the skittles once they've been knocked down. He said that he'd like to come back up again because all of us are quite different when we're up here than we are when he sees us down in the village. That shows that we must let our hair down a bit when we're playing. It makes us really happy to be part of the village life. We came to this house twenty-nine years ago. We didn't want to come at all because we had lived thirty-two years in our old home. But once we had come here we were happy. Dorset is a wonderful county and Dorset people chuckle and laugh through everything. They're really friendly too. And this part of the world has everything in a small way. I don't know why anybody bothers to go away for holidays from here when you've got the downs and the cliffs, the sea and the Chesil Beach, Abbotsbury and the other villages. The weather's wonderful too and, whoever you are, you'd have to be happy here.'

After school on the same afternoon, the village children come up to Norburton Hall for a Christmas Punch and Judy show presented by Sylvia Knightsmith. This party performance has become an annual fixture in Burton Bradstock: 'The puppets arrived in the family over sixty-four years ago when Nick was only a little fella of about one year old. Daddy went to Hamleys and bought the Punch and Judy to entertain us, because he'd had one when he was a small boy. After those early times I don't remember it being used at all until I was quite grown up and we dug it out to show to the Brownies. From then on it was used a few times and then put away again in the attic. What made me get it out again about seventeen years ago after Daddy had passed away I don't remember. But since that time I've used it quite a lot for the local children. We used to have a small, very old table theatre and it's still beautiful. But then a kind friend decided that we needed a bigger and better one and he made it possible. It's lovely but I declare we have to fetch out the Navy to move the thing. The children seem happy with it anyway. When the Brownies first started coming up we entertained them with my fox terrier. He was clever and used to do a circus, climbing ladders, wearing a ballet frock and things like that. Alas, we haven't got him any more and, after he'd died, I think that's probably why we got out the puppet theatre again, to do a show for the children.'

The youngsters roll around on the floor of the entrance hall and laugh as Mr. Punch throws a bowl of flour over Judy. They look on with a mixture of excitement and horror as the crocodile comes and grabs Punch by the leg. And they rush up to the little proscenium as balloons are distributed to all of them at the end. Then they file into the dining-room for a massive tea with cakes, jellies, sweets and eclairs galore: 'If you have a funny mind that has refused to grow up and if you like playing games with children, it's not a bit difficult to give a party like this. I could do a much more sophisticated show I suppose, but my simple one seems to please the audience. My father always used to give an elaborate performance, but I've been asked to leave out the hangman and the coffin scenes 'cos they might scare the children. I can't think why really because they see much worse on the television. But they're very appreciative when they come up here to the house and I love them in all circumstances. I suppose I'm a wasted mother really.'

The downstairs windows of the big house are full of light and small, smiling faces as dusk falls. In the garden an owl joins in with the excited cries of the children as they finish their tea and chase one another round the spacious rooms.

THE Chesil Bank has been famous for centuries for its smuggling and for its shipwrecks. Boats of all shapes and sizes have trawled, traded and travelled along its length. Ron Berry from Chickerell is in a proud and long line of boat-builders in the area. He has been making them out of oak and elm for the last

Ron Berry continues the craftsmanship of a long line of boatbuilders in the area around Chickerell.

forty-four years and, at his peak, used to turn out with his team five clinker-built boats a week: 'I must have built thousands and thousands of boats in my time and I've had orders from all over the world. Years ago I could build a clinker-built dinghy a day on me own. That was going some, I must say. I've built bigger boats too – forty footers and that. But they take a bit longer of course. Nowadays I'm repairing 'em more than building. I've never done so much mending in me life. Years ago I wouldn't touch a repair job. I just built all new, you see. These times you do anything you can though. The boat I'm working on at the moment I built here thirty-five years ago. Now we're putting seven new ribs in here and two new planks. Then she'll last another thirty-five years I hope without nothing being done to 'er again. As for my bigger boats, they'll last at least a hundred years I should say. They need to be strong because of the state of the sea off this coast, especially in the race round Portland Bill. That's where the rough seas are. It's where some of the best fish can be found too. These bass boats work off there in giant seas. When the wind's up you get it very bad out indeed – absolutely wicked. Most of my dinghies were lobster pot boats working off the Chesil Bank. Some of 'em are on moorings down in Weymouth. But mostly they just chuck 'em on the beach, use 'em each day to fetch in the lobsters and then leave 'em out there again when they get back. Trouble is now finding the wood we need. Oak's all right still. But we're struggling for elm. You can't get it anymore. There's none in England. The elm we're getting now is coming from Scotland and that's the last. When it's gone I dunno what we'll do. I don't think we'll get any more. And that'll be the end of it. It's sad because it's grand wood.'

The workshop is filled with the smell of resin and wood-shavings, sawdust and paint. Ron, solid, healthy and strong, saws narrow ribs and then planes them smooth. He works with the ease learnt through years of painstaking experience. Outside, a giant rusty metal tube bubbles and boils over a bonfire fed by rejected pieces of wood. Inside the pipe the narrow strips of oak are steamed until they are pliable and can be bent without breaking into the inside shape of the old boat: 'You have to steam the ribs or they'll snap when you fasten them into place. The elm bends on its own without trouble. You cut the planks to shape and just fit and fix them in. But the oak is more brittle and needs the steam. Then we use copper nails to hold the wood. They're soft and they don't tighten, you see. They don't leak and they'll last for hundreds of years. Copper don't rot in the salt water. It's the finest material of the lot for this job. I'm really proud of the work I do and of the materials I use. They call my boats the tanks of the sea because they last forever, put up with any weather and will take you round the world if you want. And they're turned out quite fast. I remember once years ago I built a motor boat for a chap. He ordered a little dinghy to go with it. It was ten foot long and clinker-built. Well, he came in on a Saturday morning and I had his motor boat ready to be launched on the Monday morning. First thing he said was, 'Where's me little dinghy?'

I told him, 'I haven't started it yet, see.'

Well,' he said, 'I'm never going to get that for Monday morning then, am I?'

I said, 'Ok, I'll start that when you go 'ome, you'll see.'

Well I began building it about twelve o'clock that day and by Monday morning the dinghy was finished and had three coats of varnish on it. Anyway, we give 'im a last coat in 'ere about five o'clock Monday morning. Then we took it down to Bridport and launched it down there and we launched the big boat as well. The owner was delighted and, in spite of our warnings, he insisted on getting into the dinghy to row out to the launch. Well, the varnish was still wet and he got good and truly glued to the seat. I don't think he ever forgot that day. It must've really stuck in his mind.'

WHEN the weather is right, Tony Hayne takes his precious pigeons down onto the Chesil Bank at West Bexington and flies them from there back to his house at Chickerell. There he runs a breeding stud for more than a thousand of the sleek, stream-lined birds. Here you will find the Shergars, the Red Rums and the Desert Orchids of the pigeon world and people come from far and wide to admire and to buy: 'There's different ways of training pigeons. It may surprise you to hear that resting them is the main thing. It's easy to train a bird and to get him fit. But it's knowing when to rest him that's most important so that he can do the job that you want him to do, whether it's sprints or middle or long distance races. Another thing that people don't know is that the cock bird's reward is seeing his hen when he comes back from a race. As soon as he comes home you can leave him with her for twenty minutes or half-an-hour if you like. You then take the hen away and he never sees her again until he next goes into his race pannier. That makes a big impression on him so, as soon as the door is opened, he comes straight out and heads as fast as he can for home and his lady friend. Winning races is what the normal club fancier is interested in. From this stud's point of view it's having birds that will breed the racers of the future. That's what we're good at and that's what we're in business here to do.'

The sound is the main thing that you notice when you visit Tony Hayne and his team. Just as the perpetual noise of the sea surrounds you on the Chesil Bank, the cooing of pigeons is your constant companion at the stud. The birds are calm and colourful as they sit comfortably on the perches in their spacious cages: 'In horse-racing you have the breeder, the owner, the trainer, the manager and the jockey all playing their part in bringing the animal to its peak. The satisfaction of pigeon-racing is that the fancier plays all those roles himself and puts his knowledge and experience into bringing the very best out of his bird and then into competing against thousands and thousands of other pigeons and the people who own them. And it's a wonderful experience, whether or not you're the winner. You see that little bird coming home after flying five hundred miles. It's racing its hardest, not just lopping along. Then it closes its wings and arrives back at your loft. There's no better thrill than that I can promise you. Your heart goes up in your mouth. Your hands are shaking to get the rubber ring off, to get it into the clock and to time that pigeon in. I don't care who you are or what you've done, it's one of the most exciting experiences you can have. Because it's you that's done it. Nobody else. And you've worked hard for it too and that's your reward. You see, a pigeon is an out and out athlete and each is an individual. You can't just treat them as a bunch of birds. At the end of the season, you can't say to yourself, 'Well, that's it for the winter' and then lock the doors. All the work that's got to be done for next year starts in September of the previous year. So your training and preparation runs from September to April when the racing season starts. That's why, if there's good weather in the winter, I take them off a few miles down the road. It's not so much to keep the body fit. It's to make the mind active all the time and to keep the homing instinct keen and alert. Of course, the training of young birds and old birds is quite different. With a young bird, to begin with, you take it just a couple of miles down the road so that, when he's released, he can see home. You do that a few times and then move him gradually further away each time – ten miles, then twenty, thirty and eventually fifty. I always let them go one at a time – single

Tony Hayne runs a breeding stud for racing pigeons close to the edge of the Chesil Bank.

tossing it's called – and not in a group. That way each one clears his own air space – then heads for home. It helps them to stay as individuals and brings out the best in them.'

Tony's responsibilities for his pigeons are weighty. He has to keep them fed, watered and cleaned, of course. They have to be housed at the right temperature and in correct numbers for each cage. They have to be recorded and watched and waited upon. They are also a financial worry: 'With some outstanding exceptions, the value of a racing pigeon goes from sixty pounds up to three or four hundred pounds. With stud birds it's much more expensive. You're talking about up to twenty or thirty thousand pounds each. Sometimes it goes a lot higher than that too. The average here I would say would be between five and ten thousand pounds. It's happened that really valuable pigeons have gone missing. They might have hit a power line or been chased by a hawk – anything like that. They get lost through no fault of their own. But, if you see one walking around the local streets, you never know how precious it may be.'

THE air along the Chesil Bank and the surrounding wide open spaces no doubt suit Tony Hayne's pigeons. To holiday-makers too the sea can seem as meek and mild and attractive as a soft summer's day. But this is a place to be treated with respect and with caution. When the wind is unleashed it can turn into one of the most dangerous places on earth, and even the great wall of stones bows before the strength of the ocean. Perhaps the ever-present threat has, over the centuries, honed and hardened the people who live along the south Dorset coast until they have become as strong, as resilient and as self-reliant as the great Bank itself.

INDEX